MBA

Japan and the Challenge of
Europe 1992

Japan and the Challenge of Europe 1992

Kenjiro Ishikawa

Pinter Publishers, London and New York

for

The Royal Institute of
International Affairs,
London

© Royal Institute of International Affairs, 1990

First published in Great Britain in 1990 by
Pinter Publishers Limited
25 Floral Street, London WC2E 9DS

British Library Cataloguing in Publication Data
A CIP catalogue record for this book is available from the
British Library
ISBN 0 86187 838 8

Library of Congress Cataloging-in-Publication Data
A CIP catalog record for this book is available from the Library of Congress.

Printed in Great Britain by
Antony Rowe Ltd, Chippenham, Wiltshire

Contents

List of Tables   vii
Abbreviations   ix
Foreword   xi
Preface   xiii

1 Introduction: A 'Single European Market' and Japan   1

2 Post-war Trade Relations between the Community and Japan   12
  Mutual misunderstandings   12
  The widening trade gap   18
  Japan's low import propensity   32

3 European Dilemmas   40
  Declining European competitiveness   40
  Defensive European responses   48

4 Agenda for Adjustment   55
  Structural reforms in Japan   55
  Quantitative restrictions – discrimination   64
  Automobiles – a sensitive sector   68
  The Nissan case – local content requirement   76
  The 'screwdriver' regulation   82

5 Towards 1992   95
  Japanese investment in the Community   95
  Reciprocity   108

6 Conclusion: The Tasks Ahead   118

Notes   127
Index   145

List of Tables

1 The macroeconomic consequence of market integration for
  the Community in the medium term   4
2 EC trade with EFTA, the US and Japan   5
3 Japanese foreign exchange reserves, 1951-7013   13
4 Japanese exports to the Community: some of the major items   17
5 Japan-Community automobile trade, 1977-80   25
6 Importers' share of the West German car market, January-
  May 1979 and 1980   27
7 Japanese car access to the Community market, June 1981   27
8 The development of trade between the Community and Japan   31
9 Japan's manufactured imports   32
10 Household saving ratio   39
11 The structure of Japan's export trade   43
12 Wage costs and productivity: annual growth rates   46
13 Changes in shares of OECD exports   47
14 Index of changes in comparative advantages in exports of
   high-technology products   47
15 Investment in manufacturing (1975 process and exchange
   rates)   48
16a. Tariff burden of selected industrialized countries and the
   Community, 1987   56
16b. Examples of tariff reduction or elimination   56
17 The process of import liberalization in Japan, 1960-86   57
18 QRs eliminated by the Japanese government in 1988   59
19 Comparison of residual QRs   60
20 Japan's imports of manufactured goods   62
21 Trade between Japan and the Community   62
22 Discriminatory QRs on imports from Japan, December 1988   64
23 Japanese car makers' market share   70
24 Registered vehicles imported into Japan, 1983-8   72
25 Abolition of national quotas without any Community
   measures   75

26 World car sales and production forecasts 77
27 Community and anti-dumping duties against Japan 93
28 Japanese direct investment in the Community (1) 98
29 Japanese direct investment in the Community (2) 100
30 Japanese direct investment in the Community (3) 102
31 JETRO's survey 1988 (1) 105
32 JETRO's survey 1988 (2) 107
33 JETRO's survey 1988 (3) 107

Abbreviations

ACP	African, Caribbean and Pacific Associates of the EEC
ANFIA	National association of motor vehicle manufacturers (Italian)
BDI	Confederation of West German industry
CBI	Confederation of British Industry
CCMC	Committee of Common Market automobile constructors
CECIMO	European committee for cooperation between machine-tool industries
CJPrint	Committee of Japanese Printers
CLCA	Liaison committee of the EC car manufacturers
CMEA	Council for Mutual Economic Assistance
DG	Directorate-General (Commission of the European Communities)
DRAM	dynamic random access memory
EC	European Community
ECU	European Currency Unit
EEC	European Economic Community
EES	European Economic Space
EFTA	European Free Trade Association
EMS	European Monetary System
EUROPRINT	Committee of European printer manufacturers
FIRA	Foreign Investment Review Act (Canada)
GATT	General Agreement on Tariffs and Trade
GDP	Gross Domestic Product
GNP	Gross National Product
GSP	Generalized Schemes of Preferences
JETRO	Japan External Trade Organization
LTA	Long Term Arrangement on cotton textiles
MFA	Multi-Fibre Arrangement
MFN	Most-Favoured Nation

MTN	multilateral trade negotiations
MITI	Ministry of International Trade and Industry (Japan)
NTB	non-tariff barriers
OECD	Organization for Economic Cooperation and Development
QR	quantitative restrictions
REI	Ricoh Electronics Inc.
SITC	Standard International Trade Classification
SIDM	serial impact dot matrix computer
TRIM	Trade-Related Investment Measure
UNICE	Union of industrial and employers confederations of Europe
VAT	value added tax
VCR	video cassette recorder
VER	voluntary export restraints
VTR	video tape recorder

Foreword

Over the past five years the Royal Institute of International Affairs has seen a steady expansion of its research activities on both Western Europe and East Asia. One welcome result has been the current emphasis of the Institute on exploring the new relationships that are developing between a European Community intent on further economic integration and its major trading partners, including Japan. Kenjiro Ishikawa completed this study as a Visiting Fellow in the Institute in 1988–9. His account of the history of Euro-Japanese trade relations in the context of 1992 provides both a carefully documented analysis of events and a stimulating Japanese response to a European venture that will undoubtedly extend well beyond its original economic goals. His interpretation, however, is his own, and the views expressed in the study are not to be taken as being those of the Institute. The Institute intends to follow this volume with other studies which will add to the range of interpretations of the way in which an increasingly unified Western Europe handles its relations with other countries.

Royal Institute of
International Affairs,
London

Sir James Eberle
Director

Preface

The envisaged completion of a single European market by the end of 1992 will increase the economic and political weight of the European Community; it has already had a considerable impact on its international economic and political role. In the light of its status as one of the strongest economic powers in the world, the Community can and should exert a constructive influence on the world trade system.

Once internal border controls and national trade restrictions have disappeared, a common external economic policy is indispensable for the Community. However, it is necessary to consider the extent to which an open single market will affect economic relations with third countries. At present, many EC member states still have in operation protective mechanisms of their own, including against Japan. When the single market is completed, these will have to be either abolished or put on a common basis.

The declaration by the European Council in Rhodes of December 1988 to the effect that 'the internal market will not close in on itself' is an important step in the direction of a liberal approach. This is the Community's first attempt at defining its external economic position in the context of completing the single market.

Concrete solutions, however, are needed for translating such declarations of intent into practice. Since June 1985 when the EC Commission launched its White Paper for completing the internal market, the assessment of the single market by third countries has ranged from concern or scepticism to positive expectation. Many third countries are concerned because they fear that what they see as the protectionist tendencies of some member states may be transferred to the Community as a whole. These fears are understandable.

As for Japan, in the thirty odd years since the signing of the Treaty of Rome, the Community has had difficulty in finding a coherent approach to solving trade problems with Japan and has consistently resorted to discriminatory measures. In the background, there have been several factors, such as a mutual lack of interest during the post-war period; lingering resentment against Japan as a result of the war; memories of aggressive Japanese trade practices in the pre-war era, and of shoddy goods, low wages, patent piracy and dumping practices. Even though the 'shoddy goods' image had long since become a thing of the past, the Community's discriminatory treatment of Japan continued.

Over the past year or two, however, there have been some positive developments in trade and economic relations between the Community and Japan. Japan has moved towards less export-dependent economic growth, reflecting precisely the kind of structural adjustments that outsiders desire, and its tariff and non-tariff barriers (NTBs) are now among the lowest of those of the major industrialized countries. These positive trends are reflected in its external trade, including trade with the Community. Its investment in the Community has also increased substantially over the past few years. As for the Community, there has also been some movement: its attitude towards Japan has become unmistakably more friendly and constructive. However, what remains to be seen is whether it will sustain a more liberal approach towards Japan beyond 1992, since its discriminatory attitude seems to be very deep-seated.

This study, which is based on Community and Japanese government documents, has two main aims: it seeks to analyse the origins of the Community's attitude towards Japan and, in particular, of its discriminatory treatment of Japan, by providing readers with the background to trade relations between the EC and Japan since the establishment of the Community; and it attempts to suggest possible future directions in which the two parties could go in the light of the 1992 programme.

The book is the product of research which I undertook as a Visiting Research Fellow at the Royal Institute of International Affairs (Chatham House) in London during 1988-9; it should be noted, however, that the views expressed in it are entirely my own and are in no way to be interpreted as being those of the Institute.

I am deeply indebted to the Institute, and to a number of its staff, for enabling me to undertake this project. My thanks are due in particular to the Deputy Director, Dr William Wallace; to the Head of the West European Programme, Dr Helen Wallace, for constant encouragement and many helpful suggestions; and to the former head of the East Asia Programme, Dr Brian Bridges, whose generous support and friendship were an incalculable asset throughout my work. I also feel greatly indebted to the members of the Chatham House study group, as well as to colleagues at the Institute, for commenting on the typescript; to the staff of the Institute's Library and Press Library for collections of materials and data; and to many friends elsewhere, including Giorgio Boggio, Guy Crauser, Dr Brian Hindley, Dr Jean-Pierre Lehmann, Christian Masset, Simon Nuttall, Danièle Smadja, Juichi Takahara, John Wilson and Professor John Zysman for valuable comments and suggstions. My special thanks go to Head of

Publications at the Institute, Pauline Wickham, for looking after the publishing arrangements so efficiently, and to Rosamund Howe for editing the text with such skill. A last acknowledgement must be made to my wife, Teiko, who consented to come to live in London again and gave me unceasing support and encouragement.

London   Kenjiro Ishikawa
July 1989

1 Introduction: A 'Single European Market' and Japan

After many years of stagnation and irresolution, the European Community (EC) has woken up to the challenge of its long-standing vision for establishing a true single European market, a 'Europe without frontiers'.

The Community has committed itself to realizing, by the end of 1992,[1] the objective of providing its twelve member states with the free circulation of persons, goods, services and capital. If all goes according to plan, there is the prospect of a market free of practically all restraints to competition. The Community will form a third capitalist economic power, encompassing the world's largest home market of 320 million people.

The concept of a single European market is already thirty years old. The idea behind the 1992 programme was enshrined in the Treaty of Rome (EEC).[2] From the 1970s into the early 1980s, the Community was lagging behind its main competitors, Japan and the United States, in terms of output growth and job creation. Its industries did not keep up with the application of new technologies; the oil crises, international recession and monetary instability all took their toll. The West European economy seemed first to be paralysed by its own 'Europessimism' and then to be crippled by 'Eurosclerosis'.

The leaders of the Community finally acknowledged that, in order to remedy these structural deficiencies, they had to go back to the original aim of the six founder member states and their Treaty commitment to establish one fully integrated market. The turn-round came in 1985.[3] The watchword has become the target date of '1992'. The panorama is changing, rapidly and substantially. The 1992 programme, more than any other European integration initiative since the Second World War, has captured the imagination of entrepreneurs, and has generated a set of expectations with real political force among the West Europeans. A number of business leaders and government officials of the member states have started to talk and act as if the 1992 programme might actually happen, might actually be more than a day-dream.

The central objective is the completion of an internal market in the Community by means of 279 legislative initiatives (whittled down from 299 originally proposed by the Commission) which were aimed at removing the existing physical, technical and fiscal barriers to the free circulation of persons, goods, services and capital. Over 90 per cent of these measures have already been tabled by the Commission, and by the end of June 1989 more than half of them had already become law.[4] A single European market seems fast becoming a reality.

But a great deal remains to be done. In general, the obstacles to be removed are numerous, the technical and administrative problems to be solved are complex and cumbersome. Many of them are made all the more intricate because of their linkages with political issues.

Take, for example, the question of how to find a compromise on value added tax (VAT); an answer to calls for a 'social dimension' (e.g. by creating a single European company statute with provisions for worker participation in management); a plan for breaking the deadlock in monetary integration by the creation of a European central bank and a single European currency; or a means to control crime, terrorism, drug-trafficking and illegal immigration as a Europe without frontiers comes closer to reality. And what is meant by European union, laid down in the Single European Act, remains an open question. Margaret Thatcher, the British Prime Minister, has dismissed the case for tax harmonization and the need for a single European company statute, is adamantly opposed to a European central bank and a single European currency, and has rejected as folly moves towards a political union of European nations.[5] This illustrates one extreme of the political arguments, but there are reticences in other member states as well which counterbalance the enthusiasm of certain others.

Most of the real arguments have only just begun, and any battle over such matters promises to be especially difficult and hard fought. No wonder some express doubts. Since the authors of the Treaty of Rome launched the original EEC in 1957, much progress towards that goal of economic integration has been made; but some ambitions have not been achieved. A number of barriers still remain between the member states; completing a single market in full will take much longer.

However, the complete realization of the programme on schedule is not what matters most. The important thing is that Western Europe is once again becoming a driving force. The path now taken can set off new forces. According to calculations in a persuasive study coordinated by Paolo Cecchini, an Italian economist, at the Commission's request, the potential economic gains of full market integration will amount to at least 4.5 per cent of the gross domestic product (GDP) of the Community.[6] However, the conclusions of this study are regarded by some as excessively optimistic, with a tendency to pay too little attention to the more difficult problems. For example, three economists from DRI Europe, a well-known forecasting organization, while foreseeing some effects on particular industries, anticipate a much smaller macroeconomic effect.[7] Even Frans

H.J.J. Andriessen, Vice-President of the Commission, admits: 'Experts may have differing views about the precise figures. As a former Finance Minister, I know only too well that no two economists ever agree'.[8]

More growth, more jobs, more income and more imports through the removal of production and trade barriers, as well as structural improvements under the pressure of increased competition: these are not just good reasons for the creation of a single European market; they also underline the need to guard against the danger of the single market becoming a closed fortress.

Now that the Community is gaining in stature and authority as a result of the 1992 programme, governments and economic circles in countries outside the Community are becoming uneasy. They are closely monitoring the Community's process of integration, are weighing up possible opportunities and disadvantages, and in some cases are keeping a lookout for suitable counter-strategies.

This is illustrated by a recent volte-face by the Communist bloc. For decades the Soviet Union had taken the stand that guidelines for trade and cooperation should be laid down in an agreement between the Community and the Council for Mutual Economic Assistance (CMEA) and that the Community's dealings with individual CMEA countries should be limited to technical matters. Now, however, it has come to accept the establishment of formal relations between the Community and the East European countries individually.

Simultaneously, the fear about a possible turning-inward of the Community as a consequence of the completion of the single market is voiced very clearly and very frequently in several Western countries, notably the member countries of the European Free Trade Association (EFTA), the United States and Japan.

EFTA is the biggest trading partner for the Community. In 1987, the two-way trade between the EC and EFTA exceeded ECU 170 billion – almost equal to EC-US and EC-Japan trade taken together (see Table 2). There are mounting fears among EFTA members that the move to complete the single European market could result in *de facto* barriers emerging between the Community and EFTA, and that their existing bilateral free trade agreements with the Community might no longer remain in force.[9] In July 1989, Austria, one of the current six EFTA countries, applied for EC membership (which promptly threw member states into some disarray on account of Austria's accompanying insistence on staying neutral forever).

Community members, for their part, are determined to ensure that EFTA does not get a free ride but makes equivalent concessions. In January 1989, Jacques Delors, President of the Commission, put the question to the European Parliament, saying: 'We have been travelling with them [the EFTA countries] along the path opened by the Luxembourg Declaration of 1984 on the strengthening of pragmatic cooperation.[10] . . . We are coming up to the point where the climber wants to stop to get his breath, to check

Table 1 The macroeconomic consequences of market integration for the Community in the medium term

	Customs formalities	Public procurement	Financial services	Supply-side effects	Total Average value	Total Spread
Relative changes (%)						
GDP	0.4	0.5	1.5	2.1	4.5	(3.2 – 5.7)
Consumer prices	–1.0	–1.4	–1.4	–2.3	–6.1	(–4.5 – –7.7)
Absolute changes						
Employment (millions)	200	350	400	850	1800	(1300 – 2300)
Budgetary balance (% point of GDP)	0.2	0.3	1.1	0.6	2.2	(1.5 – 3.0)
External balance (% point of GDP)	0.2	0.1	0.3	0.4	1.0	(0.7 – 1.3)

Source: HERMES (The Commission and national teams) and INTERLINK (OECD) economic models, in The Commission, *The European Challenge 1992 : The Benefits of a Single Market*, Brussels, 1988.

Table 2 EC trade with EFTA, the US and Japan (mECU)

	Import		Export	
	1985	1987	1985	1987
EFTA	82,011	82,679	84,711	90,287
Iceland	580	722	606	685
Norway	17,716	12,106	9592	9512
Sweden	19,595	20,056	20,812	20,192
Finland	7570	7873	6454	7014
Switzerland	23,688	26,696	29,220	32,772
Austria	12,861	15,226	18,087	20,112
United States	68,942	56,213	85,523	71,899
Japan	28,586	34,757	10,475	13,618
Intra-EC	466,742	459,706	466,594	486,836
Total	874,742	829,134	849,936	829,911

Source: Eurostat, *External Trade*, Luxembourg, February 1989.

that he is going in the right direction . . .,'[11] and he outlined two options:

- we can stick to our present relations, essentially bilateral, with the ulti-mate aim of creating a free trade area encompassing the Community and EFTA;
- or, alternatively, we can look for a new, more structured partnership with the common decision-making and administrative institutions.[12]

This means that it is up to EFTA to strengthen its own structure so as to make such a link with the Community possible. For, as Helen Wallace and Wolfgang Wessels point out in a recent study, whereas relations between the two parties are of great importance for EFTA countries, they matter rather less for Community members, for whom the 1992 programme, and relations with the United States and Japan, take precedence.[13]

The United States, too, is concerned that the emerging single market could discriminate against third countries or cause the EC to seek to extract concessions from its trade partners. It is worried about possible 're-ciprocity' rules restricting, for example, financial services provided by firms owned outside the EC; local content standards affecting imported cars and other goods; and controls of mergers and acquisitions. In particu-lar, that reciprocity, above all 'mirror-image' rules, would be used as an instrument of protectionism.[14]

The Commission has stated that it will seek reciprocal treatment by their markets from countries outside the Community as a condition for access to the integrated market in services, investment and other areas not covered by the General Agreement on Tariffs and Trade (GATT). As of March

1989, reciprocity provisions have been incorporated into the proposals for a Second Banking Coordination Directive;[15] for an Investment Services Directive;[16] for a Directive on Life Assurance;[17] and for two Directives on procedures for the award of public contracts.[18]

The Commission, which is still in the process of formulating policy on the implications of 1992 for countries outside the Community, has yet to provide a precise definition of reciprocity. It does, however, reject criteria based on the 'mirror-image' test, and has given an assurance that reciprocity does not mean that all partners should grant the same concessions, or that the Community requires concessions from all its partners;[19] instead it stresses that 'reciprocity must be understood in the sense of equivalent reciprocity (equal treatment) rather than identical reciprocity.'[20]

The United States, in its Omnibus Trade Act, enacted in August 1988, warns that it might close its market to firms from countries which discriminate against imports from the USA. On 25 May 1989, the US government decided to put four member states – Italy, Greece, Spain and Portugal – on a special watch-list under the Super 301 provisions of the Trade Act as candidates for possible future retaliation in respect of alleged general protectionism; neither the Community nor any member states, however, were singled out as priority targets under the Super 301 or the Special 301 provisions that relate to intellectual property trade issues. Senator Lloyd Bentsen, Democratic chairman of the Senate Finance Committee, warned that the United States might have to consider 'mirror' retaliatory action if the Community increased trade barriers against the United States as a result of the single European market.[21]

Finally, there is also concern in political and economic circles in Japan that the single market will create barriers to commerce and investment that are broader, more systematic and more damaging than the scattering of measures that already hinder some aspects of trade between Japan and the Community. These worries stem partly from Japan's overall assessment of the current international political and economic situation.

First of all, it is clear that the international situation now is different from that of the late 1950s, when the Treaty of Rome entered into force. Recently, there has been a tendency towards protectionism – whether unilateral or bilateral – in the industrial countries, which has begun to undermine the free trade regime that had developed under US leadership after the Second World War around GATT. A single European market could well encourage unilateralist or regionalist developments; moreover, there are several EC member states with old protectionist habits.

Secondly, the motive behind the idea of creating a single European market is conspicuously different from that of establishing the European Communities in the late 1950s. When the movement towards an integrated Europe started in the late 1940s, it was activated by the political and economic decline of the European countries in the 1930s, followed by the Second World War; the perception of a Soviet threat; and the desire to overcome past divisions. Japan hardly came into it.

In the post-1985 era of a declining Soviet threat in Western Europe, the Community is faced with the economic might of the United States and Japan, as well as changes in political and security relations across the Atlantic. Undoubtedly, one of the motives behind the 1992 programme is the revitalization and strengthening of Western Europe's ailing economy so as to provide an effective means of competing with the giant resources of the United States and, especially, Japan. No wonder Japan feels uneasy.

The root causes of the Community's threat to the present trading system may be identified as follows: its propensity to work out bilateral and sectoral deals; its tolerance of discriminatory practices which are particularly burdensome to Japan and developing countries not affiliated with it; and its structure and decision-making process.[22] Japan, in point of fact, has been the object of sustained discrimination at the hands of the Community since its establishment.[23]

The evidence here is clear. In the 1950s, when the question of Japan's accession to the GATT arose, several present member states of the Community invoked Article 35 of GATT. This meant that GATT Article 1, mandating non-discrimination, was not to be applicable to their trade with Japan, nor would they give most-favoured nation (MFN) treatment to Japan. In the early 1960s, the invocation was removed, but Japan had to accept the inclusion of selective safeguards in bilateral agreements with these countries, as well as later various discriminatory export restraints, in particular the so-called 'voluntary' export restraints (VERs).

Even now, there are still long-standing quantitative restrictions (QRs) which individual member states of the Community are authorized to maintain against imports of certain products, principally from Japan and Eastern Europe. Although they have gradually reduced such restrictions on Japanese products, and the United Kingdom had totally eliminated them by the end of 1967, as of the end of 1988 some 131 nationally imposed restrictions remained on 107 products.[24] In March 1989, the Commission notified Japan that it would lift 42 of these QRs in the near future, but its proposal does not include such major Japanese export items as cars, motor cycles and electric household appliances[25] and will hae no major impact on overall Japanese exports to the Community.

These QRs are discriminatory and many of them remain in force for what appear to be political, rather than economic, reasons. Even the Commission feels that the maintenance of these national regimes, and the subsequent partitioning of the market that they imply, would not be compatible with the objective of integrating the member states' economies within a single European market.[26] For this reason, the Commission envisages that the 'completion of the single market will mean the removal of QRs and will require unified import rules in respect of non-Community countries'.[27]

Japan is therefore expecting that some QRs will be maintained also after the completion of the single market, even if under a different regime. Its manufactures are accordingly intensifying their direct investments in Western Europe and expanding their cooperation with European partners. Entrepreneurially, this is the right answer to QRs.

However, another conflict, on the Community's local content requirements, is already approaching. These require that foreign-owned firms use a minimum percentage of production inputs for goods made in the Community. They are the EC's response to Japanese firms' moves to circumvent anti-dumping duties through the establishment of so-called 'screwdriver' assembly plants in member states. In the autumn of 1988, for example, the French government claimed that cars made at the UK assembly plant of Nissan Motor, Japan's second largest car manufacturer, did not qualify as Community products because their local content amounted to less than 80 per cent of their total value.[28] The cars would consequently become subject to France's import quota.

But both Nissan Motor and the British government insisted that the cars should have free access to the West European market, since they had a local content of 70 per cent, well in excess of the 60 per cent level widely argued as the minimum for cars to qualify as Community products.[29] Nissan Motor also expressed its hope of reaching the 80 per cent level by 1990.[30] By April 1989, it seemed clear that France would climb down, but the principle is still far from resolved.[31]

A related and equally crucial issue arises from the Community's new anti-dumping regulations for parts and components under which the Commission may impose anti-dumping duties on goods mainly produced by Japanese plants in the Community. The regulations are aimed at Japanese companies which have so far avoided anti-dumping penalties on finished products by setting up 'screwdriver' assembly plants which merely assemble dumped components imported from Japan. Since the new regulations took effect in June 1987, the Commission has opened investigations into a number of Japanese assembly plants in the Community and imposed anti-dumping duties on their products.[32]

There is, however, no clear evidence that the Commission has properly assessed whether the components were being imported at dumping prices, or that it has substantiated 'injury' to European producers. Nor is it clear whether the Commission was requiring that too high a percentage of the components be locally manufactured. Incorrect application of regulations of this type could sharply reduce the benefits of the integrated market to countries outside the Community.

The 'reciprocity' issue which the Community claims in fields such as financial services has also worried Japan, because, until at least several years ago, Japanese investment has been concentrated in the financial sector. There are as yet no internationally accepted regulations governing the services trade, since these are only now being discussed at the Uruguay round of the GATT multilateral trade negotiations.

As mentioned earlier, the Commission defines 'reciprocity' as 'a guarantee of similar – or at least non-discriminatory – opportunities' for firms from the Community to operate in foreign markets on the same basis as local firms.[33] This was intended to answer foreign fears that the Community might demand treatment exactly 'mirroring' the freedom of a single European market. But confusion and concern still remain.

The Community indicates that this reciprocity must be understood according to a 'global' conception,[34] and explains that 'overall reciprocity means a balance of mutual advantage'.[35] In principle, global or overall reciprocity appears to be based on a bilateral and sectoral balance of advantages.

In today's world, different legal and social systems exist for many justifiable reasons in different countries, and it is difficult to produce a workable definition of reciprocity. If it were taken to mean a withdrawal of a benefit each time the other country could reciprocate, the scope for free trade would be considerably limited. This point will be analysed in detail in Chapter 5.

The Community, describing what is meant by a single European market, uses the image: 'l'Europe ni forteresse ni passoire' (Europe neither fortress nor sieve), and points out: 'the internal market will not close in on itself. In 1992 Europe will be a partner and not a 'fortress Europe'. The internal market will be a decisive factor contributing to great liberalization in international trade on the basis of the GATT principles'.[36]

However, there is a gulf between theory and practice. As mentioned above, there is a strong trend towards reinforced protectionism in the Community, especially against Japan. On quantitative restrictions, for example, the Commission is striving for the removal of national QRs. But as the Commission itself has indicated,[37] it does not rule out Community-wide restrictions in areas designed as 'sensitive'. There are also fears that member states with the most conservative position on this issue may effectively dictate policy.

In the automobile sector, for example, the European industry wishes to insist that the Community should help it by holding off Japan;[38] however, in May 1989 the Commission proposed the abolition of bilateral import quotas used by France, Italy, Spain, Portugal and the United Kingdom to protect their car producers against Japanese competition.[39] But French and Italian manufacturers, who are strongly protectionist, argue that the local content of a Japanese car made in the Community should approach 100 per cent.[40]

Community member states which advocate this sustained discrimination against Japan could call on a range of justifications. From the 1950s to the 1970s, the West Europeans feared Japanese trade practices such as exporting shoddy goods, low wages, and trade mark and patent piracy. However, by the 1980s, their complaints had substantially changed, to centre on the strong Japanese work ethic, government support to industry, quantitative and qualitative restrictions – which have become famous as non-tariff barriers (NTBs) and the sizeable and virtually permanent visible trade surplus, against the Community in particular.

During the post-war period, Japan's domestic market was almost closed. At this time, it suffered from a chronic shortage of foreign exchange. Its balance of payments tended towards deficit until the late 1960s. At the time when the Community was established, Japan did not constitute a market which could absorb many European products: in the 1950s, GNP per head in Japan corresponded to less than a third of that of the Community. As a result, the Japanese government had to give priority to policies designed to develop domestic industries and modernize the country at the expense of expenditure on private consumption.

Japan's export policy in the 1960s and the 1970s was far more successful than the government had expected. In a period of scarcely twenty years, Japan changed from being a country manufacturing 'shoddy goods', the low cost-price of which depended mainly on low wages, to being a highly industrialized country, both a major consumer of capital and a highly competitive economic giant. Aware of this situation, the Japanese government began to move towards gradual integration into the world economy. It steadily liberalized tariffs, quotas and investment restrictions.

The opening of the Japanese market coincided with the enormous increase in Japan's trade surplus. Since the beginning of the 1970s, the Community's trade deficit with Japan has regularly increased. Moreover, Japanese exports to the Community were concentrated into a limited number of sectors which were directly hit by this intense competition: electronic products, sound and television equipment, automobiles and motor cycles. Conflict was inevitable. European criticism started by focusing on Japan's determination to penetrate Community markets. Then, after Japan introduced VERs, the emphasis shifted to the galloping trade imbalance and the impenetrability of the Japanese market with its restrictions and technical or administrative impediments.

The Japanese government has taken steps to meet these complaints, but its corrective measures have been implemented slowly or in a piecemeal fashion, following the usual tendency of Japan's trade policy to evolve through consensus between opposing interest groups and also respond to outside pressure, from the United States in particular. Following more or less continuous change, it cannot now be argued that Japan enjoys low labour costs, an under-valued currency, low capital costs or high tariffs.

The Community's criticism vis-à-vis Japan has gradually changed. In a statement of 25 April 1988, the Council actually welcomed structural reforms taking place in Japan and observed that Japan's economic performance and international economic trade relations were moving in the desired direction.

Since the mid-1980s, there have been several positive developments in economic relations between the two parties. Until 1985, with the exception only of the oil crisis years, Japan's exports grew consistently faster than its GDP. Since 1986, however, domestic demand has been the most important determining factor for Japan's economic growth. This trend has naturally been reflected in its external trade statistics, with the Community in particular. In fact, Japan's imports from the Community have been growing faster than its exports to the Community every year since 1986.[41] The pace of Japanese direct investment in the Community is accelerating, although its favourite destinations still appear to be neighbouring Southeast Asian countries and the United States. Moreover, in addition to its well-established technological cooperation with the United States, Japanese high-technology firms and industries have been moving rapidly towards closer ties with the Community.

Andreas van Agt, head of the EC Commission of Japan, said: 'We are both now exporting more to each other than ever before. In fact, the Community is the only part of the world with which Japan's two-way trade is growing'.[42] He has also stated: 'Japan is considered now by us Europeans as an opportunity. . . . We no longer regard our relations with Japan as pertaining to trade figures and trade figures alone'.[43]

There are still a lot of fundamental problems to be settled, however. Both the Community and Japan have to make further efforts to improve their economic relations. For example, while the Community appreciates Japan's structural reforms and general economic performance, it would like Japan to depend more on its domestic market and to extend its structural reforms. Japan retains some national features such as oligopolies and a complicated and expensive distribution system which hinder foreign firms' access to its market.

However, the Community must make sure that the 1992 programme does not give rise to discriminatory and protectionist trade policies, vis-à-vis not only Japan but also other countries outside the Community. Fortunately, there are signs that liberal attitudes are starting to prevail. On 2 December 1988, the European Council in Rhodes declared that: 'The internal market will not close in on itself'. On 13 April 1989, the Commission tried to inject more flexibility into the treatment of non-Community banks in its proposals for a Second Banking Coordination Directive (see below); and in May 1989, it proposed the abolition of national import quotas against Japanese cars and ruled out the creation of specific Community local content rules.[44] These moves are important steps towards a liberal approach, and it is imperative that they should be translated into practice, though numerous hurdles remain.

2 Post-war Trade Relations between the Community and Japan

Mutual misunderstandings

The world economic order established after the Second World War and based on the Bretton Woods arrangements underwent major change in the 1970s when a new trilateral relationship between the United States, Western Europe and Japan emerged. Two oil crises in the 1970s heightened awareness of global economic interdependence, and international economic cooperation has become a significantly more important factor for global economic stability and development. However, while the United States and the Community, and to lesser degree perhaps the United States and Japan, have developed wide and diversified links, relations between the Community and Japan, the third side of the triangle, are still underdeveloped. It is not simply a matter of the persistent economic and trade imbalance. There are other, more deep-rooted problems such as the vast geographical, historical and cultural differences between the two parties and also their different pattern of post-war development.

Western Europe and Japan are thousands of miles apart in geographical and cultural terms. While the culture of Western Europe is based on principles of democracy and Christianity, which it shares with the United States, Japan does not follow the same system, at least not in the international arena. Moreover, since the Second World War, the West European countries and Japan have moved in different directions. Europe was divided politically and geographically. The West European countries were severely weakened, and had to devote all their energies to post-war economic rehabilitation and to their colonial and security problems. Japan, which was occupied by the United States for seven years after the war, also concentrated on economic reconstruction.

The West European countries developed the Atlantic partnership with the United States and moved towards some form of integration in Western Europe. Japan was of little importance to the West European decision-makers, who gave it fairly marginal attention. There was mutual lack of interest. Western Europe saw Japan as a semi-developed country with a

Table 3 Japanese foreign exchange reserves, 1951-70

Year	$m	Year	$m
1951	930	1961	1486
1952	913	1962	1841
1953	637	1963	1878
1954	738	1964	1999
1955	839	1965	2107
1956	941	1966	2074
1957	524	1967	2005
1958	831	1968	2891
1959	1322	1969	3496
1960	1824	1970	4399

Source: Ministry of Finance of Japan. The figures for 1951 to 1955 are to the end of the fiscal year, and for 1956 to 1970 to the end of the calendar year. After 1963 the figures exclude IMF gold tranche.

closeted market and aggressive export practices.[1] But Japan had lost its vital traditional markets on the Chinese continent through internal political upheaval there and through US hostility towards Communist China in the long post-war period. As a result, Japan also turned to the United States for its overall – not only economic, but political, security and cultural – re-lations. Western Europe's moves were of little concern to Japan, although most West European countries resumed diplomatic relations with Japan after the conclusion of the San Francisco Peace Treaty in September 1951. Underlying Japan's lack of interest in and inadequate understanding of Western Europe was a tendency to underestimate it.

However, Western Europe's lack of interest in Japan was much more serious. In addition, there was still very strong resentment against Japan in many West European countries as a result of the Second World War. They remembered aggressive Japanese practices in the pre-war era and were still afraid of Japanese low-wage products, trade mark and patent piracy, and dumping practices.[2] All these factors fostered a discriminatory attitude against Japan after the war.

In 1952, Japan formally applied for GATT membership but faced strong opposition from the United Kingdom and British Commonwealth countries such as Australia and South Africa. It was only in 1955, with the support of the United States, that Japan was accepted into the world trade body as a contracting party. But even when Japan became a GATT member, fourteen countries including a number of major West European countries such as the United Kingdom, Belgium, the Netherlands and later France refused to extend MFN treatment to Japan, citing Article 35 of the Agreement. Among the West European countries, only West Germany and Italy granted MFN status to Japan, while the Netherlands accepted an MFN relationship with Japan in a bilateral agreement.

When Japan applied for GATT membership it needed extensive export opportunities because the decline of the Korean War boom after 1953 meant that it was short of the foreign exchange it needed for importing food, raw materials and machinery for economic reconstruction. Foreign exchange reserves fell from $930 million in 1951 to $637 million in 1953 (see Table 3). But Western Europe was not in a position to accept Japan as an equal partner in either the political or the economic field. The West Europeans feared an aggressive export offensive from Japan. One of the reasons behind the West European opposition to granting Japan MFN status was to prevent Japanese goods, cotton textile products in particular, flooding their markets. People still remembered how Japan had dumped its goods in world markets in the 1930s, for example, the so-called 'watches by the kilogram', and how it had flooded the US market after it was opened to Japanese textile exports. These feelings were described in an article by James Meade:

[The United Kingdom] was influenced by memories of the nineteen-thirties when many existing lines of trade and production were disrupted by a sudden incursion of cheap Japanese products, sold in many cases by means of questionable commercial devices which misled customers about the origin, content or quality of the goods, which relied upon the copying of other traders' designs and which involved export subsidies. . . .[3]

Citing Article 35 of the GATT was the first discriminatory measure against Japan to be adopted by West European countries after the war. Other such measures have continued ever since.

Japanese interest in West European markets was aroused by the establishment of the EEC in 1958 and EFTA in 1960. Japan feared that European integration and the development of economies of scale would make West European industries more competitive and more threatening to Japanese industries. At the fifteenth plenary session of GATT member countries in Tokyo in October 1959, and through bilateral negotiations with the major West European countries, Japan tried to have Article 35 of the Agreement abolished and so get out of the impasse it found itself in.

In 1963 the United Kingdom became the first West European country to withdraw from the application of Article 35 against Japan, following the conclusion of a bilateral Treaty of Commerce, Establishment and Navigation. The Treaty replaced Article 35 by two safeguard clauses, under one of which each country could impose selective restrictions on imports of the other's goods, if they caused or threatened serious damage to domestic producers. It was just before the conclusion of the treaty that Norman MacRae wrote his famous article 'Consider Japan' in *The Economist*, pointing out: 'They could beat us competitively in a much wider field of industry than most people in Britain begin to imagine', and 'British economy has lessons to learn from Japan, not the other way round'.[4]

Following the United Kingdom, in 1964 France and the Benelux countries stopped invoking Article 35 against Japan, which, however, had to accept the same safeguard clauses as it had concluded with the United Kingdom. In addition, West Germany and the Benelux countries removed substantial restrictions against Japanese imports. West Germany conceded MFN status to 80 per cent of its imports from Japan under a trade protocol of 1956;[5] and the Benelux countries granted Japan *de facto* MFN status in 1960. In 1964, Japan was admitted to the Organization of Economic Co-operation and Development (OECD).[6] Without these developments Japan might not have been able to confront the intractable problem of unilateral discriminatory measures against it in Western Europe.

These developments indeed proved to be a turning-point, and trade relations between Western Europe and Japan gradually improved. Both parties, Japan in particular, experienced remarkable economic expansion for the next decade, until the first oil crisis in 1973 threw the world economy into turmoil. During this decade GDP in the West European countries except the United Kingdom increased by 4.5 to 5.5 per cent annually; meanwhile the average annual growth rate of Japan's GNP was around 10 per cent, twice the rate of Western Europe.[7]

Japan's growth resulted mainly from its highly expansive economic policy and very successful development in areas with a particularly high potential for international growth, especially metal-processing industries and chemicals. Japan's automobile industry, a key industry in modern economies, could serve as a model for other countries. In 1958, the year the EEC was established, the Community produced three times as many (384,000) commercial vehicles as Japan (138,000); but ten years later, in 1968, Japan produced three times as many (2 million) as the Community (634,000). Production of other motor vehicles in Japan rose from 50,600 units in 1958 to over 2 million in 1968; but in the Community only from 2.6 million to 6.3 million.[8]

Following the Second World War, Japan, wishing to achieve a healthy balance of payments like any other developing country, had to sacrifice the import of consumer goods in order to import the raw materials and equipment vital for the re-establishment of its industry. But in 1964 its overall balance of payments went into credit, and showed a handsome surplus of $1,600 million in 1968. Japan's foreign exchange reserves rose from $831 million in 1958 to $2,891 million in 1968, and then jumped sharply to $18,365 million in 1972.[9] The pressure on its balance of payments was progressively eased.

Trade between Western Europe and Japan also expanded rapidly. Exports from the nine-member Community to Japan increased from $198 million in 1958 to $899 million in 1968 (Japanese imports from the Community from $211 million to $1,025 million). Community imports from

Japan also increased from $241 million to $987 million over the same period (Japanese exports to the Community from $256 million to $1,103 million).[10] Apart from Libya, Japan was the country which expanded its trade with the Community most rapidly over this period. But Japan was still of little significance in the Community's external trade: in 1968, only 2.1 per cent of all exports from the Community to third countries went to Japan, and imports from Japan constituted only 2.1 per cent of total imports from third countries.[11] The Community's volume of trade with Japan was less than its trade with Spain, Switzerland or Sweden.

But distrust of Japanese export strategies was deeply rooted and fears persisted about market disruption due to Japanese imports. A number of Japanese products were still subject to QRs, and many of these restrictions did not apply to imports from other countries. In September 1970 the number of restricted items still amounted to 65 for Italy, 61 for France, 27 for the Benelux countries and 23 for West Germany, although many states had reduced them several times during the 1960s.[12] The French attitude was conspicuously tight. It used several protectionist measures against Japan, including Article 35 of the GATT with a threefold increase in the maximum tariff. It also applied rigid import quotas. It was only at trade talks between the two countries in early 1964 that France became rather more prepared to ease restrictions.

West Germany and the Benelux countries imposed purely nominal restrictions. In 1965 Japan's actual exports of the restricted items were well below the quotas. The QRs, therefore, no longer restricted Japanese exports significantly and had become almost meaningless. But even though Japan insisted that the restrictions operated by other EC members were discriminatory and contradictory to MFN principles, most of them were maintained.

The common commercial policy of the Community was due to come into effect on 1 January 1970, from which date all trade agreements with third countries were to be concluded on a Community basis.[13] In December 1969, however, the Council authorized member states to renew or extend certain existing trade agreements and treaties with third countries provided that they did not constitute an impediment to the common policy.[14] In this context the member states declared that the maintenance of such agreements need not be an obstacle to the opening of negotiations at Community level with the third countries concerned.[15] Afterwards, the Community also adopted a new version of the rule allowing member states to maintain some national measures. This mainly affected Japan.[16]

Early in 1970, Japanese exports to the Community began to accelerate substantially: from $1,380 million in 1969 to $2,229 million in 1971 and $3,305 million in 1972 (see Table 4). A real imbalance became evident. This trend is indicated by the import/export cover ratio, which declined from 85.9 per cent in 1969 to 69.9 per cent in 1971 and 59.3 per cent in

Table 4 Japanese exports to the Community: some of the major items (¥ bn)

Item	1970	1975
Automobiles	17	191
Ships	70	120
Radios	19	83
Television sets	—	34
Office equipment	—	60
Optics	42	131

Sources: Japan Statistical Year Book, 1971, 1976, Bureau of Statistics, Office of the Prime Minister, Tokyo, 1972 and 1977.

1972.[17] In addition, Japanese exports to the Community were concentrated into a handful of specific and increasingly sensitive sectors such as the radio and television, tape-recorder, the other electronics, ships, and automobile and motor cycle industries (see Table 4). This substantial increase in Japanese exports to the Community began to cause serious problems for the corresponding industries in the Community. In addition, some leaders of West European industries warned that the West European countries could expect a 'concentrated penetration' of their domestic markets by Japanese goods diverted from the United States following President Nixon's economic measures.[18]

Attempting to allay European fears, leaders of the Japan Federation of Economic Organizations (Keidanren) made a tour of several West European countries and held out the prospect of what they called a programme of 'orderly marketing' including the series of 'voluntary self-restraint' agreements on exports, a highly convenient method of trade restriction.[19] The offer was made at a meeting with the Commission on 25 October 1971 and also at another meeting with delegations of the Union of Industries of the European Communities (UNICE) and the Confederation of British Industry (CBI) on the following day, both in Brussels. The joint communiqué issued after the meeting between the Keidanren, the UNICE and the CBI stated:

to prevent a return to protectionism . . . the Community delegation has considered it absolutely necessary for the Community to adopt a safeguard mechanism designed to forestall the risk of market disruption. For its part, the Keidanren delegation described its conception of orderly marketing which would have as its objective, by means of voluntary regulation of exports, the harmonious development of trade.[20]

The leaders of the Keidanren explained that Japan would be prepared to work out VER agreements for certain products such as steel, provided that the Community would give up its idea of a permanent safeguard clause in the framework of the planned overall trade agreement between the Community and Japan.[21]

The first VER after the Second World War appears to have been agreed between Japan and the United States on cotton textiles, then Japan's principal export product. This VER became the Short-Term Arrangement regarding International Trade in Cotton Textiles; it then developed into the Long-Term Arrangement (LTA), and finally the Multi-Fibre Arrangement (MFA), with its thousands of quotas on exports of specific products from specified sources to designated destinations. As for the West European countries, the first VER was adopted when the European and US steel industries privately negotiated a 'self-limitation' agreement in 1968.

Following the Keidanren's initiatives, Kakuei Tanaka, then Japan's Minister of International Trade and Industry, announced in April 1972 that Japanese electronic manufacturers would set VERs on tape-recorders, television sets, electronic desk-top calculating machines and several other products, to avoid an economic war with Western Europe. Then in June 1972, the Japanese electronics industry decided to apply price controls to its exports of television sets and other household equipment to the Benelux countries.[22] Three months later it extended this price control to the export of television sets and tape-recorders to eight European countries: the United Kingdom, Sweden, Finland, Denmark, Switzerland, Ireland, Portugal and Italy.[23] Similar restrictions were further extended over a broad range of sectors from electronic calculating machines (the Community) to colour television sets (the United Kingdom), ball-bearings (France and the United Kingdom), iron and steel products (the Community) and automobiles (the United Kingdom).

It should be pointed out, however, that VERs are contrary to Article 19 of the GATT. This article authorizes emergency protection in the case of a serious threat to a domestic product. It stipulates that any government taking such action must consult exporting governments. It has also been interpreted to require that any restrictions imposed should be non-discriminatory,[24] since, though Article 19 does not state that the restrictions should be non-discriminatory, Article 1 of the Agreement matinains the general principle of non-discrimination. The Commission, together with some member states, the United Kingdom and France in particular, very much wanted to modify Article 19 so that it could be applied selectively.[25] They would then no longer have to rely on 'self-limitation' agreements, which were then the only way for the Community to check Japanese imports in the absence of an official trade agreement between it and Japan. But the Commission, of course, realized that the modification would change the fundamental character of the article so as to permit discriminatory action against one country or group of countries which was considered to have caused or threatened serious injury. Any such modification would put certain Japanese exports at a disadvantage compared with the same exports from other countries. As a matter of principle Japan opposed the modification and insisted that any restriction ought to be applied only after evident market disruption.

Questions were also raised as to the compatibility of VER agreements with both Community and West German rules of competition. The West German government and the Commission were highly critical of the large number of bilaterally negotiated VERs. In July 1972, the Federal Cartel Office in West Germany declared that such agreements to restrict competition on the West German market were illegal as they kept prices up artificially.[26] Then the West German Economics Ministry pointed out that even voluntary restrictions on imports would be seen as running counter to both West German and Community laws of competition, and dismissed all such restrictions as 'fundamentally undesirable'.[27]

The Commission, in an effort to retain some political control over the increasing number of such agreements between West European and Japanese manufacturers, took steps to bring them under Community control,[28] and then published an opinion on the subject.[29] The Commission's view was that such agreements might well contravene the free competition provisions (Article 85, para. 1) of the Treaty of Rome, which prohibited market-sharing operations. It considered that such agreements, apart from their possible effects on 'free competition, were under neither member-government nor Community control, despite the fact that the Commission was supposed to be in charge of the Community's common commercial policy. Under the Commission's plans, companies were required to notify the Commission of any 'self-limitation' arrangement they intended to make. Notification was also compulsory in cases where companies in the Community were not involved but sales inside the Community were affected.

Consequently, in November 1973 the Commission opened official proceedings against a VER agreement concluded between French and Japanese manufacturers of ball-bearings but not endorsed by the two governments.[30] The Commission said in an official communication to them that the manufacturers were suspected of infringing the free competition provisions of the Treaty of Rome and asked them to explain their case.

The Commission was in a difficult situation because member states differed widely in their attitudes to the rising tide of Japanese exports of certain specific products. West Germany favoured united negotiation of a trade agreement by the Community but pursued a much more liberal import policy, as its government did not favour self-limitation agreements. France differed from West Germany on some counts: it was highly protectionist and feared that united Community negotiations might damage its substantive interests.[31] It used sovereignty arguments to insist on negotiations taking place between governments. The United Kingdom differed from both France and the Benelux countries by pursuing a liberal import policy, and from all these countries and West Germany by preferring negotiations to take place on a private basis, from industry to industry. In addition, the Commission itself divided the task between the Directorate General (DG) for Competition and the DG for External Affairs. While the former tracked down agreements concluded by industries without government involvement, the latter sought to reduce national government participation in external trade matters.[32]

Even Japanese ministers pointed out this inconsistency in the Community attitude several times. For example, Nobuhiko Ushiba, then the Minister for External Economic Affairs, complained about being forced to deal with the Commission:

What kind of authority they have and what they are up to, I really never could make out in my visits to the Commission itself. Now we have to negotiate with the Commission, because the Commission has overall competence over economic negotiations. But in fact the Commission cannot move at all without being given a mandate from the participating member countries, and the Commission has no authority to tell the member countries to do anything.[33]

Following this criticism of the Commission, Kiichi Miyazawa, then the Director of the Economic Planning Agency of Japan, said:

The Commission gets its authority from the member countries of the Community but in the background are the demands of all member countries, among which some are important and some are not important to each of the countries. In general, the Western Europeans, except for West Germany, have the disposition of a Kyoto confectioner. When a problem occurs, it may be fine to speak out loudly in a businesslike way as the United States does, but that isn't going to solve the problem quickly (for Western Europe).[34]

'Kyoto confectioner' is a reference to the small shopkeepers of Japan's old capital who make no effort to sell their cakes and sweets but sit quietly in their shops waiting for customers to come.

These fundamental differences between member states and within the Commission itself, and also the absence of an official trade agreement with Japan on a Community basis, meant that the Commission could not do anything positive. At that time, the member states were linked commercially with Japan by bilateral agreements of varying content including safeguard clauses.

The widening trade gap

The Commission started negotiations to conclude a trade agreement with Japan in Tokyo in September 1970. These were the first major trade negotiations the Commission had conducted on behalf of all member states under its common commercial policy. Japan had long complained of being subject to unequal and unfair trade treatment by some West European countries. In the early spring of 1970, it had taken part in negotiations with Italy and France to seek the removal of these allegedly discriminatory provisions. It was worried that the Community might seek to insert a safeguard clause in a common trade agreement.[35]

As Japan expected, the Commission indicated at a preparatory meeting in February 1970, held with a view to exploring the possibilities of entering into official negotiations, that in any agreement reached with Japan the Community would insist on safeguard clauses to prevent a sudden flood of Japanese goods into Western Europe.[36] It demanded that such a safeguard clause should apply generally to all items to be imported by member states from Japan. The Commission was told by member governments that it must secure a safeguard clause of equivalent strength to those provided for the then bilateral agreements between Japan and France and the Benelux countries.

Japan, however, refused to accept even the principle of a general safeguard clause that could cover every product it exported to the Community. It argued that the rules of the GATT already provided sufficient protection for the Community, so no additional measures were required. For largely political reasons, Japan seems to have wanted not to be the only member of the GATT to be singled out for such treatment. But Japanese anxieties were equally great in the strictly commercial field. If the Community negotiated a general safeguard clause, an important precedent was going to be set for relations with Japan's other trading partners, the United States in particular.

To try to avert such a threat, and to meet at least part of the Community's demands, Japan came up with a number of compromise suggestions in its talks with the Community. One of these was a somewhat vague undertaking to stick to the principles of 'orderly marketing' in trade with the Community. Another proposal was that the Community should apply Article 19 of the GATT, which allows member states to take action to protect their markets in certain circumstances.[37] Japan also offered a further suggestion that the safeguard clauses already operated by France and the Benelux countries should be extended to the other Community members, West Germany and Italy, but the clauses would not apply to products as and when they were liberalized on a country-by-country basis.[38]

The Community, and particularly France and the Netherlands, remained adamant that safeguard measures should remain permanent and global.[39] The Commission still wanted to insert a safeguard clause in a common trade agreement.[40] But the Japanese government again declined the offer, stating that it was well capable of handling its conflicts with Italy and the Benelux countries by itself without such an agreement.[41]

There was an almost psychopathic fear of Japanese competition in some business sectors in the Community. It was true that Japanese exports to the Community were steadily mounting, and since around 1972 in particular a

Japanese sales offensive had been in full swing. Japan's exports increased by 43.8 per cent in 1972 and 33.5 per cent in 1973, while the corresponding figures for Japanese exports to the United States were 17.9 per cent and 6.6 per cent respectively. Key Japanese exports aroused protectionist feelings in Western Europe.

There were several reasons for the expansion of Japanese trade to Western Europe and the Community in particular. First, the new economic policy adopted in August 1971 by Richard Nixon had the effect of intensifying pressure for restraint on Japanese exports to the United States. Since the 1950s Japan had gradually increased its share of the US market for labour-intensive consumer goods such as ceramics, cutlery, textiles and precision-mechanical goods. Japan then found itself able to conquer the market for more capital-intensive consumer goods and also for some investment goods such as computers, electronic apparatus, automobiles etc. This trend was quantifiable in the USA's trade deficit with Japan: $604 million in 1968, $923 million in 1969, $451 million in 1970 and $2,634 million in 1971.[42] All the more reason for President Nixon's new economic policy to be a shock to Japan. As a result of and following the first oil crisis, Japanese demand was on the downturn. This led to a fall in production targets, and then a stagnation of economic growth such as Japan had not known since the Second World War. These circumstances undoubtedly stimulated a Japanese drive to diversify exports and seek new outlets in Western Europe. This was a market which until then had been neglected because it was separated from its Japanese competitors by two continents and two oceans, and because it had formidable NTBs, mainly a variety of discriminatory quotas, to stem the tide of Japanese goods. Nevertheless, from the toe of Italy in the south to the bluewater shipbuilding ports of Scandinavia in the north, Japanese industries were having an impact in Western Europe.

However, it was not until late in October 1976 when a Japanese industrial delegation led by Toshio Doko, then President of the Keidanren, visited the United Kingdom, West Germany, France, Denmark and the Commission of the European Communities that the West Europeans raised their voices in unison. The Japanese realized that its advocacy of free trade would not move the West European countries, where some six million people were unemployed. Hence the speedy action by Japanese industries, encouraged by their government. However, even before the industrial leaders' visit, Japan had begun to take notice of the West European demands for better access to its market and had simplified some of the more rigid requirements of Japanese law.

An important case in point was a decision taken by the Japanese government in May 1976 to smooth the way of West European cars after a long period of strong protection.[43] Among various concessions being offered to the West European car manufacturers was an agreement that safety and pollution checks on their export models should be carried out in the Community rather than in Japan as hitherto. West European car manufacturers had complained that testing their export models in Japan was often costly and cumbersome; they had to ship their models to Japan, sometimes only to find that they did not satisfy Japanese inspections and had to be sent back for modification.

As a result, immediately after the industrial leaders' visit to the West European countries, Japan took action to ease its trade surplus with the Community and defuse what was becoming a serious political issue:[44] Japanese car exports to the United Kingdom in 1976 would not significantly exceed the level of 1975; Japan, though thinking it most useful to continue multilateral consultations, agreed to hold bilateral meetings with the Community to discuss its share of the shipbuilding industry; and Japan would take steps to increase its imports of Community skim-milk powder for feed use.

Nevertheless, Japanese exports to the Community continued to increase rapidly, without a corresponding increase in Community exports to Japan. The trade gap between the two parties widened further. This again began to cause acute tension even though the Community, or rather the Commission, subscribed to the principle that countries should balance their accounts with the outside world on a multilateral, not a bilateral, basis. The Commission noted in a working paper:

The bilateral surplus of Japan with the Community does not constitute in itself, in a multilateral world, a cause for complaint. We [the Community] have for example now a very substantial trade surplus with countries such as Austria, Australia and Yugoslavia and that is why we would not be satisfied if the countries concerned adopted counter-measures.[45]

Moreover, in the 1970s the Community's overall balance-of-payments situation was not notably weak. Its current account was in surplus several times during that decade. Some billion dollars' deficit in its bilateral trade account with Japan, therefore, should not have mattered. What did matter was that the Community's deficit with Japan was becoming larger every year. The Commission repeatedly attributed this trend to Japan concentrating its exports into a few specific industrial sectors while keeping its own imports of finished goods at an artificially low level, that is to only one-fifth of its total imports.

However, the Japanese Ministry of Finance claimed in a confidential report that the Commission's arguments were misleading.[46] To the Commission's complaint that Japan was bombarding specific industries in the Community, the report made this reply:

Car and steel exports to the Community were 11.2 per cent and 5.6 per cent respectively of Japan's total car and steel exports to the world in 1975. As a share of total Japanese exports to the Community, cars were 13.8 per cent and steel was nearly 7 per cent. Do such levels represent what the Japanese poetically term *shuchu gou*, or 'concentrated rainfall', of cars and steel on the Community market?

On the problem of Japan's finished goods imports, the report started by admitting Japan's dependence on imported raw materials, and insisted that this dependence was far greater than any other industrial country. Then the report pointed out that the low level of finished goods imports was largely because Japan was not surrounded by other industrial countries. It argued that if, for instance, intra-Community trade was excluded, the share of finished goods in Community imports fell from 55 per cent to only 38 per cent; and if trade with other European neighbours and members of the OECD was also excluded, only 31 per cent of Community imports were finished goods, while Japan's level was 19.9 per cent in 1975.

However, Wilhelm Haferkamp, the Vice-President of the Commission responsible for External Relations, made the following criticism of Japan's attitude at a press conference in Tokyo in March 1979: 'As long as Japan enjoys surpluses of this magnitude, we think that Japan has a special responsibility towards her trading partners to eliminate or lower existent restrictions. And we do not like the idea of negotiating every year with the same list of specific complaints.'

This language was the bluntest yet to be used in public in the Community's long-standing trade dispute with Japan. Immediately after, the Commission in Brussels leaked a notorious working paper which described Japan as 'a crowded, highly competitive island only recently emerged from a feudal past' and 'a country of workaholics who live in what Westerners would regard as little better than rabbit-hutches . . .'[47]

The Commission's tone was hardly surprising because after the 1979-80 round of oil price increases, the world economy slowed down again, with the Community and the United States in particular going down the slippery slope of recession. Japanese competition in Western Europe was again perceived as one of the main threats to the Community. Especially disturbing was the increasingly protectionist attitude to those industries which had traditionally depended on free trade.

In the United States, domestic manufacturers laid off thousands of employees at a time when Japanese cars were continuing to pour into the country. In May 1981, the Tokyo government was forced to limit exports of Japanese cars to the United States by 7.7 per cent and to Canada by 6 per cent from the 1980 levels for the next three years. In Western Europe, there were already formal or informal curbs on the import of Japanese cars to the United Kingdom, France, Italy and Spain. But Japanese export penetration rose in West Germany and other West European countries. Pressure for controls at Community level therefore gained ground.

Japanese car sales to the nine-member Community jumped 29 per cent from 585,824 units in 1979 to 765,000 units in 1980, lifting their market penetration from 7.9 per cent to 11.1 per cent (see Table 5). At that time,

Table 5 Japan–Community automobile trade, 1977-80

Year	Registration in Community of passenger cars imported from Japan	Percentage increase	Japan's market share of total registrations in the Community (%)
1977	467,896	16.3	6.8
1978	511,422	9.3	6.0
1979	585,824	14.5	7.9
1980	756,000	29.0	29.0

Source: Japan Automobile Manufacturers' Association, *Japanese Passenger Cars Registered in Europe*, 1982.

there was already over-capacity in the Community market and the French Peugeot group (which includes Citroën and Talbot), BL of the United Kingdom, Fiat of Italy, General Motors in the United Kingdom and Ford in West Germany were all piling up substantial losses. Several assembly plants had been closed in Scotland (by Peugeot), England (by BL) and Belgium (by Renault, Citroën and BL). It was alleged that an influx of Japanese cars had contributed to the closing of the plants in Belgium.[48]

Ford of Europe pointed out in a report submitted in September 1980 to the European Parliament that increased car imports – mostly from Japan – by the nine member states could cost 133,000 Community motor industry jobs by 1985; this could mean a total job loss of 560,000, including indirect employment.[49] In October 1980, Bernard Hanon, then Managing Director of Renault, the nationalized French car corporation, called for a bold and aggressive protectionist policy to prevent Japanese car exports flooding the Community market. He said:

Action is needed because Japan indulges in unfair competition, in that she is fifteen years behind her competitors in terms of giving social benefits to workers, and since Renault exports more than half its output, it cannot afford to be protectionist in outlook. But trade with Japan is exceptional because of the way imports are shut out. Renault produced two million cars in 1979, but was only able to export 500 cars to Japan.[50]

In June 1981, the French motor manufacturers' association attacked a plan by Nissan Motor to set up a car factory in the United Kingdom, saying Japanese penetration of the West European market was already excessive and must be limited. It said it had no objection to Japanese firms operating in Western Europe if they used West European components and labour almost exclusively, but this condition was unlikely to be fulfilled in the United Kingdom project. Then André Giraud, at the time French Industry

Minister, accused the British government of lack of Community solidarity in its decision to back the establishment of the Nissan car plant in the United Kingdom.[51] Nissan's plan, announced on 29 January 1981, was to build a plant in the United Kingdom producing 200,000 vehicles a year for sale throughout Europe by 1986.[52]

Later, it became clear that since July 1980 the French government had been refusing to allow Japanese cars to be transported from the docks to showrooms without special licensing arrangements, and thousands of Japanese cars were being held in French ports. Japanese car registration in France had jumped 28.8 per cent from 42,625 units in 1979 to 54,897 units in 1980, increasing their market penetration from 2.2 per cent to 2.93 per cent.[53] But Japanese manufacturers complied with an unofficial limit by which their share of total registrations in the French domestic market was not to rise above 3 per cent. The French government had been operating this policy through 'administrative guidance' since 1977, and the Japanese government regarded it as effectively constituting an import restriction. The Ministry of Foreign Affairs lodged a strong protest against what it claimed to be 'undue discrimination' against Japanese car exports to France, saying that:

The French government has withheld giving type certificates for new Japanese cars since July 1980, making it impossible to sell them in France. If this move is aimed at keeping Japanese cars' share of the French market within 3 per cent, it constitutes undue discrimination against Japan, which runs counter to the spirit of the GATT.

Meanwhile, the Council, the European Parliament and the Commission issued statements on 2 May 1981 saying that exports of Japanese cars to the Community should be subject to a limitation analogous to the one decided by Japan vis-à-vis the United States.[54] About a month later, West Germany, Belgium, Luxembourg and the Netherlands joined the chorus of demands for greater restraint by Japanese car exporters. The Japanese nearly doubled their share of the West German car market in the first half of 1980 (see Table 6), and the impact of this was exacerbated by a surprisingly sharp fall in demand for new cars. Car production in West Germany fell by 9 per cent in the first six months of 1980 to 1.97 million vehicles, compared with 2.16 million in the first half of 1979. The main slump came in the domestic market where registrations of new cars fell by 13 per cent in the first six months of 1980 to 1.39 million, and a growing share of these sales went to the Japanese.[55] In these circumstances, Japan agreed to keep the annual growth rate down to 10 per cent.[56] It also agreed to curtail its 1981 car shipments to Belgium and Luxembourg by 7 per cent from the 1980 level and to hold exports to the Netherlands to the 1980 level (see Table 7).[57]

This ominous escalation of trade restraints against Japan by several West European countries was followed by an even sharper deterioration of

Table 6 Importers' share of the West German car market, January-May 1979 and 1980 (%)

Country	Jan-May 1979	1980
Japan	4.7	8.7
France	10.5	10.0
Italy	4.4	4.2
United Kingdom	0.5	0.4
United States	0.6	0.3

Source: West German Motor Industry Federation, July 1980.

Table 7 Japanese cars' access to the Community market, June 1981

Italy	2,000 units annually
France	Share held to 3%
United Kingdom	Share held to around 11%
West Germany	10% annual growth rate
Belgium/Luxembourg	7% reduction on 1980
Netherlands	Held at 1980 level
Denmark, Ireland	Open

Sources: Europe, 12/13 January 1981; The Commission, *Imports of Japanese cars to the EEC and the US,* 2 May 1981; *The Financial Times,*11 June 1981; and *International Herald Tribune,* 12 June 1981.

trade relations when the Community adopted a special system to monitor Japan's sales of sensitive products (such as motor vehicles, certain machine tools and colour television receivers and tubes) to each member state.[58]

On machine tools, the Commission pointed out that, through the systematic application of new technology and a highly original development strategy, Japanese machine tool manufacturers had had a determining influence over the recent development of industry; their share of exports had jumped to 43 per cent in 1979 from 27 per cent to 1975.[59] However, according to the European machine tool confederation (CECIMO), the Japanese only had a 3 per cent share of the Community market.[60] Nevertheless, CECIMO asked its Japanese counterpart for restraint in the development of Japanese exports to the Community, and had the Commission introduce an arrangement for monitoring machine tool imports.

In about 1980 growth in the world market for colour television receivers and tubes was reduced and competition among manufacturers increased by the Japanese offensive in particular. The Japanese industry regarded the

Community market as attractive, because ownership of colour television sets was still low in the Community compared with Japan and the United States. In 1980 the number of colour television sets per 100 households was 138 in Japan, 108 in the United States, and only 63 in the Community.[61] Even in West Germany ownership was only 65 per cent – the highest in the Community – followed by 60 per cent in the United Kingdom and 35 per cent in France. Japan was putting the Community industry under increasing pressure, especially in West Germany, one of the few countries without any restraint on imports at that time.

The profits of European manufacturers, mainly Philips of the Netherlands, Europe's biggest television manufacturer, and Thomson-Brandt of France, had been falling. According to Philips's annual report, overall pre-tax profit fell by 12 per cent in 1979 from the 1978 level.[62] Philips responded by markedly cutting production in its electronic com-ponents and glass division in the Netherlands. It considered that it needed a number of years for restructuring and claimed that the Japanese VERs were not working, so that a quota system as applied by the United States was necessary.[63]

However, the two companies' real reason for demanding a quota system was reportedly that they were both keen to consolidate their position in the West German television market. They agreed that if the Community were to introduce quotas for Japanese products, it could protect Community manufacturers against Japanese export competition.[64] Philips had a 25 per cent stake in Grundig, its largest outside customer for tubes and West Germany's biggest television manufacturer. Thomson controlled the tube operation of AEG-Telefunken and bid for SABA, both West German electronics manufacturers.

Early in 1983, the Community struck another blow against Japanese electronics products. This mainly affected video tape recorders (VTRs) and followed controversial French measures against imports of Japanese VTRs and anti-dumping proceedings by Philips and Grundig against Japanese VTR manufacturers. Late in October 1982, the French government announced that all VTRs exported to France had to pass through the tiny customs post at Poitiers, 210 miles from Paris,[65] although most imports went through customs in Le Havre or the Paris region. Imports would require documentation in French and the identification of the country of origin. Even individuals bringing recorders in their luggage would have to send them to Poitiers. The result was that clearance slowed down sharply. It was estimated that at most 2,000 units a week were getting through, and during the two months until mid-November 1982 only 16,000 recorders were cleared, compared with the 150,000-200,000 expected by importers.[66] On 10 November 1982 *The Financial Times* reported:

France is experiencing its first rationing queues for more than 30 years as the video-hungry line up in stores, desparately demanding the latest supplies of video recorders. Stories of scuffles and sit-ins at big Paris shops as stocks dwindle have left the Socialist government unmoved. Fewer than 6,000 are to be released from government customs warehouses in the Christmas period instead of the 200,000 ordered to fill an aching cultural gap.

Of course Japan issued a strongly worded request that the French government withdraw these measures.[67] It pointed out that although the measures were not exclusively directed against them, Japanese manufacturers stood to suffer more than others from one measure in particular: the ruling that all imports of VTRs should be cleared through a single customs office in Poitiers.

The French government came under strong attack from the Commission and other member states. The Commission warned France that unless it lifted its customs restrictions on imports of VTRs and abandoned new language rules affecting all imports, it would face prosecution in the European Court of Justice, on the grounds that the measures breached the free-trading rules of Article 30 of the Treaty of Rome.[68] Count Otto Lambsdorff, then West German Economics Minister, criticized the French measures bluntly, saying that the French government was embarking on a dangerous course, since protectionist action of this kind would certainly produce reprisals on the part of its trading partners.[69] At the same time, some members of the French government were also threatening to block imports from other Community countries.

In response, the French government maintained that the measures were legal and in no way protectionist. It rebuffed the accusations, citing internal studies on import curbs used by its trading partners. Michel Jobert, French Foreign Trade Minister, said on 10 December 1982 that the Commission had 'gone astray' and added: 'The failure of the Community to establish regulations that have long been requested by the member countries is responsible for today's problems'.[70] He also alluded to Count Lambsdorff by claiming that the dogmatic liberalism preached by many was in fact the subtlest form of protectionism, namely that of absolute power by the stronger over the weaker. Count Lambsdorff, of course, strongly refuted Jobert's remark, saying that the so-called non-dogmatists sought to protect their own industries and jobs from imports.

The French government also pointed out in an internal administration study on restrictive practices among member states that:

[Britain] relies on country of origin labels on certain textiles, shoes and certain household electrical goods at the retail stage, voluntary restraint arguments, 'buy British' publicity campaigns and customs formalities. It is still too early to judge how effective these campaigns are as they grow more numerous and sophisticated, but there is a striking resemblance between them and some of the recent French initiatives.
[Italy] still uses residual import quotas, import deposit schemes and customs procedures.

[West Germany] and [Denmark], the countries 'reputedly most liberal', make most use of technical qualifications and standards.[71]

As a result of all the criticisms, the French were forced to withdraw the harsher and more extreme measures of protection, including the requirement for inspection at Poitiers.

Under pressure from the French government and the Community electronics industry, Philips and Grundig in particular, Japan was forced to restrain exports of VTRs and television tubes to the Community.[72] Under a bilateral agreement, Japan undertook to limit sales of VTRs to the Community for a three-year period, with a ceiling on sales for 1983 of 4.55 million sets. This compares with 1982 exports of an estimated 5.5 million sets, including nearly 600,000 knock-down kits. As a result, Philips and Grundig were guaranteed a sale of 1.2 million units in 1983.[73] It became possible for both in effect to set the price which the Japanese, the most efficient producers, had to charge for their VTRs, thus penalizing the customer.

This deal, of course, faced growing criticism from a number of member states and journalists in the Community. The West German government in particular was less than happy about the deal, and according to the *International Herald Tribune* of 21 March 1983 government sources said: 'For the most part it is designed to protect European industries from normal Japanese competition, which in our view is dangerous. The more industries in the Community are protected the less competitive they will be'. *The Financial Times* argued in its leading article on 15 February 1983:

There is a real danger of preserving a high-cost European industry which is able to compete inside the EEC because the market is rigged in its favour, but cannot compete against the Japanese in other markets. This is the crucial point. A 'fortress Europe' policy in electronics and other supposedly strategic sectors may bring short-term gains to hard-pressed European producers, but Europe still has to export to the rest of the world and such protection can only inhibit the drive for international competitiveness.

However, there was no real change in trade figures between the Community and Japan. A certain moderation of Japanese exports of sensitive products to the Community was observed, and the Community's exports to Japan grew slightly faster than imports. But the gap widened still further in the early 1980s, except during 1982 (see Table 8).

Though gradually increasing, Japan's imports from the Community continued on a fairly minor scale, accounting for less than 7 per cent of total imports in the early 1980s. The bulk of Japan's overall imports consisted of raw materials and agricultural commodities, neither of which it bought from the community on a significant scale. The Community noted repeatedly that Japanese imports of manufactures had gradually increased but remained well below those of its main trading partners (see Table 9).

Table 8 The development of trade between the Community and Japan ($m)

Year	The Community			Japan		
	Imports from Japan	Exports to Japan	Balance	Exports to the Community	Imports from the Community	Balance
1975	6344	2802	−3532	6010	3410	+2600
1976	7775	3064	−4771	7988	3658	+4330
1977	9810	3563	−6247	9914	4267	+5647
1978	12,094	4798	−7296	12,103	6154	+5949
1979	14,326	6397	−7929	13,346	7598	+7192
1980	18,558	6383	−12,175	17,286	7911	+9375
1981	17,350	6457	−10,893 (EC-10)	18,834	8566	+10,268 (EC-10)
1981	19,491	6609	−12,882	19,815	9068	+10,747
1982	19,385	6521	−12,868	18,105	7496	+10,159
1983	19,977	6851	−13,125	19,457	8577	+10,880
1984	20,953	7444	−13,509	20,165	9800	+10,363
1985	22,689	8049	−14,640 (EC-12)	21,128	9371	+11,757 (EC-12)

Source: IMF, *Direction of Trade Statistics Yearbook, 1975-81, 1981-87*, Washington, D.C.

Note: The figures for 1975-81 apply to the EC-10, although Greece joined the Community in 1981; the figures for 1981-5 apply to the EC-12, although Spain and Portugal did not become members until 1986. The discrepancies between the European and the Japanese figures reflect differences both in reporting years and in reporting methods.

Table 9 Japan's manufactured imports (as % of total imports from trade partner)

Trade partner	1978	1979	1980	1981	1982	1983	1984	1985	1986	1987
EC	86.3	83.3	86.4	85.6	86.1	85.3	84.6	84.2	85.5	85.6
USA	41.4	42.3	44.1	45.3	47.4	50.2	52.0	55.2	60.7	56.1
World total	26.7	26.0	22.8	24.3	24.9	27.2	29.8	31.0	41.8	44.1

Source: Japanese Ministry of Finance, *Boeki tokeiei* (Trade Statistics).
Note: Manufactured goods are as defined in the Standard International Trade Classification (SITC), Sectors 5 to 9. There are differences between Community and Japanese statistics.

In 1984, Japan spent $32,800 million on importing manufactured goods, which represented 23.8 per cent of the total value of imports and 2.7 per cent of GNP. The Community spent $138,000 million, 44 per cent of the total value and 6.3 per cent of GNP; and the US $231,900 million, 65.7 per cent of total imports and 7.8 per cent of GNP.[74]

Japan's low import propensity

Against this background, the Community gradually imposed a change in member states' strategy towards Japan. It gave most of its attention to putting pressure on Japan to open up its 'closed market' for imports of manufactured products. Even then several stories of successful Western pene-tration of the Japanese market were told, but mainly in Japanese studies:[75] for example, Imperial Chemical Industries, Shell, Beecham, Hoechst, Siemens, Olivetti and Air Liquide.[76] The Commission in 1985 itself admitted that visible import barriers in Japan, such as tariffs or QRs, were by then generally modest and did not constitute a real barrier to penetration of the Japanese market.[77] The Community sought, therefore, to attribute the fundamental causes of the trade imbalance to 'Japan's low import propensity'.[78] According to the Commission, this propensity was based on 'the protracted and unpredictable technical certification and registration pro-cedures and above all the habits and attitudes bred of Japan's vertically and horizontally integrated industrial, commercial and financial groups'.[79]

These procedures and attitudes became famous as 'informal barriers' or 'quasi-NTBs'. It was first pointed out in the late 1960s that the domestic market in Japan had been unfairly and deliberately protected from foreign competitors by complex NTBs.[80] In December 1969, the Commission noted that it would be necessary for Japan to open up its market to West European exports and investments by dismantling a whole range of NTBs.[81] Parallel understandings were then reached between the United States and Japan, and between the United States and the Community, to the effect that the removal of NTBs, along with tariff reductions, should be promoted within the framework of the multilateral trade negotiations (MTN) of the GATT.[82] Such measures, however, made little impact either in the Community or in Japan. But ten years later, the Commission created uproar in Japan by making the same analysis as it had in 1969:

It is difficult to accept massive Japanese surpluses, if the Japanese market is not open and if Japanese exporters, like soldiers sallying forth from a fortress, create chaos in concentrated industrial sectors of the Community having major problems on the regional level and on the employment level. If it is desired that the import-export ratio in bilateral exchanges improves progressively and regularly, Japanese imports of manufactured products will have to undergo very rapid growth. This will require structural adaptations that will permit not only the Community but also the United States and other supplier nations to sell more manufactured products to Japan. Japan has to develop policies aiming at encouraging imports.

If it would not constitute by itself an absolute answer, the opening of the Japanese market will nonetheless be essential to the pursuit of our energetic efforts to eliminate administrative obstacles.[83]

In April 1982, the Commission representative to the GATT in Geneva complained to Japan that there had been no substantial progress in opening the Japanese market, since Japan was still using other 'invisible or elusive' measures to bar imports of Community goods in violation of international trade treaties; proceedings should be taken under Article 23 of the GATT. This was in spite of the fact that Japanese tariffs conformed to the GATT rules.[84] A year later, the Community brought this case to the GATT, seeking the setting up of a working party by the contracting parties of the trade body.[85] The Community's complaints about the difficult access of manufactured products to the Japanese markets were summarized in its paper as follows:

- A great number of unnecessarily complicated, over-administered rules, regulations and standards, many of which are in substance outdated and unreasonable; as well as objectively unjustified requests for repetition of tests which had been already performed by first-class testing institutions and which are generally accepted everywhere else.
- What the Jones Committee Report of the US Congress of September 1980 terms 'cultural bariers to imports' or 'private sector quasi-NTBs'. These include attitudes and structures in day-to-day business which make it more difficult than in the Community or elsewhere for the outsider to come in; big business groupings; vertical affiliations of large, medium and small firms ('Keiretsu'); peculiar trade financing

and credit access; lack of independent dealerships in certain sectors; interlocking 'dictatorships'; a great number of industry and business associations – partly formed under government auspices – which tend to take on regulatory functions in some aspects similar to the medieval Guilds in Europe; and collective defence reactions against newcomers from outside.[86]

These complaints related to some specific features such as distribution channels; administrative guidance; government and state monopoly procurement practices; standards and testing requirements (for health, environmental and safety requirements); customs practices and so on.

(a) The distribution system

The Community pointed out that one of the most difficult aspects of the Japanese market was its 'involved and complex distribution system', which 'is often directly or indirectly controlled by Japanese producers' and 'constitutes an obstacle to the marketing of imported products, particularly of consumer goods',[87] though it is non-discriminatory in the sense that the same channels distribute both domestic and imported products. The Community's criticisms may be summarized in the following points:

(i) because of the distribution channels' length, complexity and closed nature, even excellent foreign products are shut out of the market;
(ii) because of the tendency of large Japanese companies to combine with smaller suppliers into industrial groups (for example the sole agent arrangements used by manufacturers to integrate their wholesalers and distributors into large groups under the umbrella of manufacturers), foreign companies are at a disadvantage;
(iii) because of the practice of limiting transaction partners to a set circle of affiliated firms, for example the formation of close-knit corporate groups around general trading companies, products from overseas have difficulty gaining acceptance; and
(iv) because of a 1974 law on large-scale retail stores and the informal administrative directives which were renewed in 1984, the establishment of supermarkets and department stores is limited and competitive foreign products find difficulty gaining entry.

In fact, these commercial systems or practices, many unique to Japan, have severely hindered foreign companies from enlarging their share of the market. For example, it used to be virtually impossible to sell to Japan without having an affiliate company doing the marketing and distribution. Consequently, the Japanese consumer had to pay a very high price for being supplied via multiple layers of wholesalers in a complex distribution system.

However, the rationality and efficiency of the Japanese distribution system should be promoted in a way appropriate to the diversification taking place in consumer needs, the internationalization of markets, and the information revolution in distribution.

Since the end of the 1970s the system has become far more flexible as a result of the Japanese government's measures to open up the market. Though traditional wholesalers still have a role to play, manufacturers have been setting up their own wholesale and retail outlets, and foreign companies have been establishing more Japanese subsidiaries and more distribution channels.

Greater efforts should be made by the Japanese government to make the working of the 1974 law as rational and transparent as possible in the light of new consumer needs and the internationalization of markets. Since the end of the 1970s, for example, the size – and productivity – of supermarkets and department stores has increased; the number of supermarkets and department stores has consequently fallen, though the Japanese distribution sector is still characterized by more retailers and wholesalers than other major OECD countries.[88]

The distribution process entered a process of modernization and simplification. There was, thus, some room for foreign entrepreneurs to introduce more positive marketing strategies or to establish new distribution channels, though there was still 'an enormous store of anecdotes by foreign businessmen who have been unable to sell their products in Japan, even when offering a superior item at a price well under what competing Japanese firms could match'.[89] Even a British newspaper argued that: 'It must be acknowledged that there is some truth in the Japanese argument that Western businessmen have often lacked flair in pinning down marketing opportunities'.[90]

(b) Administrative guidance

The Community's concern has also focused on government regulations in Japan, since these allegedly made it difficult for foreign goods to penetrate the Japanese market. According to one definition, administrative guidance is 'a process that consists of a government ministry's giving suggestions or advice to private business or public organizations over which the ministry has regulatory jurisdiction'.[91]

A Community document[92] arguing that the Japanese government exerted pressure on industry to limit foreign imports said that the 'Japanese Ministry of International Trade and Industry (MITI) and other ministries have in the past kept a close regulatory eye on business sectors requiring either protection or development and this has meant excluding importers' products in the same sphere'. The document cited the following:

Currently in the field of high-speed integrated circuits (ICs) there is considerable involvement of government with industry to find and produce the latest product of this technology. Since this is a sensitive area, imports are extremely difficult to achieve. However, direct government pressure to stop imports is very much less than it used to be. This is primarily because it is considered that Japanese industry is sufficiently modernized and competitive to be able to stand on its own feet against worldwide competition.

It is fairly certain that the Japanese government, mainly MITI, actively fostered competition in exports while shielding its own markets from foreign goods, but only in the period of economic reconstruction after the Second World War[93] or when time was needed to develop a local product.[94] The OECD described this process in *Japan – Economic Surveys, 1985*, as follows:

Government policy has played an important role in fostering key microelectronics industries, especially at the initial stage of development. Indeed all OECD countries directly or indirectly assist and promote their electronics industries.

Before 1971, access to Japan's market was generally limited by import quotas. Foreign direct investment in strategic areas (notably semiconductors and computers) was restricted, effectively preventing foreign firms – which had a technological lead – from entering. At a formative stage, the domestic market was reserved for Japanese industry. From 1971, however, successive measures of trade and capital liberalization were taken.

(c) Other barriers

The Commission has identified the following NTBs: taxes; public procurement; standards, testing and certification procedures; import procedures; intellectual property rights; services; and labelling.

On public procurement, the Commission complained repeatedly that:

- the Japanese authority has only made limited efforts to buy foreign products. Most purchases coming under the GATT code on government procurement have involved direct contracts, and import penetration has been low.
- other difficulties derive from tight deadlines for tenders and deliveries, complex qualification procedures which vary according to the body concerned, deposit requirements etc.
- as a result, foreign suppliers' access to Japanese public contracts has been hampered or discouraged.[95]

The Community has also argued that: 'Despite Japan being a signatory to the GATT code on technical barriers in trade, foreign exporters have run into a large number of difficulties.'[96] It has pointed out numerous specific items, in particular:

- the development of technical specifications peculiar to the Japanese market and the low level of Japanese participation in international standardization bodies;
- the lack of transparency and, in some cases, the ambiguity of regulations, leaving the public authorities a wide margin of discretion;
- over-meticulous examination and certification procedures;
- non-acceptance of tests carried out in exporting countries, so that long and costly examinations have to be repeated in Japan; and
- the total ban on certain imports on health or plant health grounds.[97]

As a result of such repeated complaints, Japan has taken a series of measures to meet the Community's demands: since 1981, to reform public procurement procedures to make things easier for foreign suppliers; to provide foreign producers with easier access to the Japanese system of standards and certification procedures; to relax money-market, capital and exchange conditions; and to give foreign financial institutions easier access to market segments.

Thus, in Japan there was certainly some use of standards, testing and certification procedures to assist local manufacturers and producers of pharmaceuticals, cosmetics, chemicals, telecommunication equipment and leather products; however, in fact Japan made very little use of such barriers to protect manufacturing industries from imports. Japan's NTBs were primarily designed to protect its agricultural producer interests and have been used mainly for that purpose.[98] The significance of the barriers seems often to have been grossly exaggerated, mainly because they tend to compare unfavourably with practices in the Community. Gary R. Saxonhouse gives a very interesting analysis:[99]

There is nothing abnormal about Japanese trade and industrial patterns . . . . There is evidence that Japan does have a distinctive trade structure by comparison with other advanced industrial economics, but only because the Japanese economy's other attributes are also distinctive. No other advanced industrial economy combines such high-quality labour with such poor natural resources at such a great distance from its major trading partners.

In this context, the Community was forced to refer to Japanese domestic institutions and even to suggest to the Japanese government that it should encourage consumer spending and discourage savings:[100]

As a result of certain social characteristics in Japan and the bias of the fiscal system in favour of savings against credit expenditure, the level of savings is very high compared to that in other major industrial countries. However, despite the relatively high growth rate in Japan domestic demand has been insufficient to absorb these savings. The result has been a large trade surplus and growing capital outflows. These imbalances indicate that there is scope for a higher level of domestic demand . . . .

It should be pointed out that in early 1985 the United States was reported to have conveyed a series of similar suggestions to the Japanese government. According to reports in the Japanese press, the United States stressed that Japan 'should counter the life styles that are deeply rooted in Japanese society'; it called for the 'creation of new financial institutions to channel postal savings capital into low-interest housing loans, consumer and import financing; tax reform to encourage consumer spending for leisure and discourage savings; and a reduction of weekly working hours'.[101]

For more than thirty years the United States and West European countries have pointed to a host of barriers in Japan which are said to have caused trade imbalances. But as Japan has gradually removed many of its most significant barriers, and as its trade surpluses have nonetheless continued to swell, the United States and then the Community have begun to stress broader macroeconomic issues, and finally 'social factors'.

In 1985, for example, according to OECD statistics, Japan's household saving ratio, or the amount saved as a percentage of household nominal disposable income, was 16 compared with 4.5 in the United States (see Table 10).

There are a number of features special to Japan which may explain this high propensity to household saving. According to OECD, these features may be summarized as follows:

(a) preparation for retirement: because the Japanese can now expect to live much longer than formerly, the proportion of elderly people in the population is growing more rapidly than in other OECD countries and saving for old age is therefore an important motivation for saving;
(b) high housing costs: the average price of a house or flat represents around ten times annual disposable income in major metropolitan areas;
(c) heavy educational expenses: the need to finance educational expenses – particularly at university level – is an important element;
(d) other factors may include the bonus payment system and tax exemption of most household interest income.[102]

It is surprising that the government of the United States or the Community could ask Japan, a 'friendly' independent country, to change its domestic institutions. In effect, both intervened in Japanese domestic affairs for the sake of their own trading performances. Yasuhiro Nakasone, then Japanese Prime Minister, said that:[103]

Japan was right in the 1950s to encourage savings by exempting the interest on most of them from tax. Developing economies need high savings to reduce dependence on foreign capital and to provide cheap cash for investment. Now Japan has more savings than it needs. The drive to save is cutting consumption and, by encouraging purchases of foreign bonds, restraining the yen's rise. It is silly that the

Table 10 Household saving ratio (%)

Country	1970	1980	1984	1985	1986	1987
Japan	17.9	17.9	16.0	16.0	16.6	16.8
USA	8.3	7.3	6.3	4.5	4.2	3.3
FRG	13.8	12.7	11.4	11.4	12.2	12.4
France	18.8	17.6	14.5	13.8	13.3	12.1
UK	9.2	13.8	10.5	9.5	7.3	5.4
Italy	30.3	28.2	24.6	24.2	23.9	21.9
Canada	5.6	13.6	15.0	13.8	11.3	9.7

Sources: OECD Outlook, No. 44, December 1988 (Japan – Economic Planning Agency; USA – Federal Reserve; FRG – Deutsche Bundesbank; France – Les collections de l'INSEE; UK – Central Statistical Office; Italy – Banca d'Italia; and Canada – Statistics Canada).

Japanese are able to spend only 58.5 per cent of their GDP on consumption, while the French spend 65 per cent; if the Japanese were encouraged to spend a bit more, they might also start buying more foreign goods.

Even if moves by the United States and the Community were not excessive, was it appropriate to ask the average Japanese family to save less and spend more, at a time when they had yet to obtain adequate housing, and to pay for their children's education, and still had a public pension system inferior to those in West European countries?

According to a report compiled by the Japanese Ministry of Construction in January 1985, the quality of life in Japan had actually suffered in the headlong pursuit of economic growth: for example, the level of social infrastructure was inferior to that of advanced Western countries; Japan clearly lagged far behind West European countries in housing stock. The report pointed out that one-tenth of the population lived in substandard housing, and floor space per house was much less than in all other advanced countries.

· It might be expected that a fall in the price of residential property in Japan would reduce the saving rate and increase investment, which would at least prevent another constraint on spending.[104] But residential housing space in Japan is in fact very limited, and the cost of buying a home has risen significantly; housing debt per employee household has increased rapidly since the 1970s. A substantial increase in investment in residential housing and a reduced saving rate therefore appear extremely unlikely. The Community would certainly welcome a greater propensity to consume on the part of the Japanese, but it is difficult to see how this could be brought about in the present domestic conditions.

3 European Dilemmas

Declining European competitiveness

Never has a country been so much criticized for its foreign trade policy as Japan. Never has a country suffered such constant discrimination at the hands of its trading partners. But never has a country been so continuously and rapidly successful in winning and expanding trade outlets.[1] These two phenomena – criticism and unfair treatment of Japan and Japanese success – have not been unrelated.

The hostile stance taken towards Japan by West European countries in particular seems to have been based on an extraordinary ignorance of the country and the survival of its 1930s image as a manufacturer of 'shoddy goods' whose low cost price depended mainly on cheap labour. Europeans have consistently regarded themselves as the teachers and the Japanese as the learners.[2] Such attitudes have proved tenacious. Even in 1978 a renowned European expert on Japan wrote that: 'When it comes to evaluating the attitude of the Japanese toward any new technology, one could compare them to eager pupils looking up to us, their teachers.[3]

There can be no doubt that at the time of the establishment of the Communities in the 1950s, West European countries had little interest in Japan. Several important factors have been cited as the original motivation for establishing the Communities: determination to prevent a further repetition of the Franco-German conflict; a need to consolidate the economic recovery of Western Europe, thereby underpinning political stability; concern over the onset of the cold war; and concern about the declining influence of Western Europe in world affairs combined with fear of the USA's and Soviet Union's rapid development of nuclear weapons.[4] Thus the primary aim of European unity was overwhelmingly political.

After the war the West Europeans urgently needed to deter the Soviet Union from any expansionist adventures in their territory. They also needed to strengthen their economic relations with each other and with the rest of the world. Walter Hallstein, first President of the Commission, pointed out that:

European civilization was threatened from the East by political forces. They were strong and growing stronger; they had vast resources; they were expansionists; they were sustained by a pseudo-religious fervour and an almost missionary zeal. Defence against them required a close-knit military alliance, firm political conviction, and the greatest possible economic strength.[5]

When moves towards a united Europe started in the late 1940s, the threat from the Soviet Union and the desire to overcome past divisions were the main driving forces.[6] Marshall Darrow Shulman pointed out that the Soviet leadership had consistently and openly expressed its suspicion and hostility towards the West before it entered into the wartime alliance with Nazi Germany.[7]

The West Europeans, however, found it difficult to achieve sustained progress towards political union. The emphasis shifted from the political to the economic arena. Meeting at Messina in Sicily on 1 June 1955, six Foreign Ministers stressed that the building of Europe 'must be achieved first of all, in the economic field', and declared that it was 'indispensable . . . to maintain her [European] position in the world, regain her influence and prestige and achieve a continuing increase in the standard of living of her population'.[8]

They were, in particular, conscious of the lack of competitiveness of West European industry compared with that of the United States. Hallstein wrote that: 'It was a shock to discover how far Europe's relative share of world production had shrunk, particularly when compared to the United States. He pointed out that:

In 1913, the countries of Western Europe had produced roughly half of the world's industrial goods. By the 1950s Western Europe's share had dropped to little more than a quarter. And, while in 1959, 69.4 million workers in America succeeded in turning out a GNP of 483.4 thousand million dollars, a labour force of 72.4 million in the countries of the European Community attained a combined gross product of 162.9 thousand million. In other words, accepting the official rates of exchange as a basis of measurement, every European produced goods and services to only a third of the value of those produced by American counterparts.[9]

Competition from large US businesses seemed unassailable to West European firms, faced with small and fragmented markets and equipped with obsolete machinery. In April 1956, Paul-Henri Spaak, then Belgian Foreign Minister, emphasized in a report submitted to the Foreign Ministers of the six founder members of the Community:

There is no motor car manufacturing firm in Europe which is big enough to take full advantage of the most powerful American machinery. No country on the continent can build large airliners without outside assistance. In the field of atomic science, the knowledge which has been acquired at great expense in several European countries equals only a small fraction of that which the United States is now putting freely at the disposal of its own industries and other countries . . .'[10]

Efficiency stemming from large-scale production was thought necessary to sustain rapid growth in Western Europe. Europeans believed it could be obtained through the economic integration of their countries. These economic benefits were recognized before the war, but post-war developments made them appear even greater.

Japan, on the other hand, had been destroyed by the defeat in 1945 and had been occupied by the United States. Its economy suffered from a chronic shortage of foreign exchange. Imports were simply an extra: it had to ensure supplies of raw materials and essential manufactured goods for as long as they could not be produced within the country. This strengthened a tendency to develop the trans-Pacific relationship with the United States. It also turned gradually to Southeast Asia for its new markets, having been deprived of its pre-war colonies – Korea, Taiwan and Manchuria. Japan became separated from Western Europe in both political and economic terms. Western Europe was itself too much occupied with its economic reconstruction to think about relations with Japan.

From the late 1950s to the early 1960s, West Europeans were beginning to become aware of the rapid growth of the Japanese economy – the 'economic miracle' of Japan. But this growth was regarded quite sceptically because Japan's image in Western Europe was still of a cheap-labour country with strong development needs, which would aggressively market its textiles and other basic products on West European markets.[11] Japan was granted little credit for its 'miracle' until the late 1960s. But even in the early 1970s, the Europeans considered Japan as only deserving attention some time in the future:

Japan will become increasingly important in future as a partner of the European Community. It is developing at such a furious pace that by the end of the 1970s it promises to have as high an income per head of population as the countries of the European Community. It is again becoming not only the centre of the East Asian economic area but indeed is extending its influence beyond that area.[12]

West Europeans were surprised at the speed and efficiency of Japan's economic expansion and feared a new 'yellow peril' with hordes of 'shoddy goods' attacking sensitive industrial sectors of Western Europe. But hardly any mention can be found in Community documents of anxieties about serious trade conflict between the two parties in the future.

When negotiations between the two parties began for a comprehensive trade agreement in September 1970 – and were proceeding far from smoothly – Hallstein expressed his hopes for success in these negotiations with 'a rising industrial power'. He seemed not to worry about the various import barriers in Japan, commenting:

This trade agreement will be the first that the Community has concluded with an industrial power. So far, the volume of trade between the two had been disappointing: 2 per cent of the Community's total trade, 5 per cent of that of Japan, 30 per

Table 11 The structure of Japan's export trade, 1930s and 1950s (in percentages of total value)

	1934-6	1954	1956	1959
Textiles & products	52.0	40.3	34.8	29.8*
Raw silk	11.1	2.9	1.7	1.3
Cotton fabrics	16.5	15.5	10.7	8.4
Clothing	–	3.4	4.9	6.0
Metals & metal products	8.2	15.3	13.6	11.6
Machinery & vehicles	7.2	12.4	19.3	23.4
Total (including others)	100.0	100.0	100.0	100.0

Source: Japanese Ministry of Finance.
*This fell to 12.5% in 1970 and 5.5% in 1978.

cent of whose trade is done with the United States. But it is growing rapidly: in 1969 the Community's exports to Japan rose by 16 per cent, and Japan's sales to the Community by 36 per cent.

Japanese protection is high: in addition to the highest tariff of all industrialized countries, it has strict quotas on imports and administrative and tax rules affecting not only the imports of goods but also capital movements and investments. But large-scale liberalization is in progress: already in 1970 it was announced that Japan hoped to halve quota restrictions by the end of 1971; in January 1971 this move was followed up; and in March 1971, after long and difficult negotiations, the Japanese textile industry declared its willingness voluntarily to limit its exports of wool, cotton and synthetic textiles to the United States.[13]

Criticism in Western Europe of Japanese trade behaviour seemed to be based mainly on memories of the 1930s, when the world economy fell into the Great Depression and Japan made an aggressive export offensive against world markets, allegedly using cheap labour. The British cotton industry in the inter-war years declined continuously, chiefly because former purchasing countries, especially India, became able to supply the bulk of their own needs. In these circumstances of dwindling international trade, British industry was very badly hit by the growth in exports of low-price Japanese cotton piece-goods.[14] At that time, more than half of Japan's exports were textiles such as raw silk and cotton fabrics, and the label 'Made in Japan' on goods such as textiles and toys became synonymous with cheap and unreliable (see Table 11).[15]

By the end of the 1960s, however, the position had changed radically as a result of Japan's new economic power and competitiveness. From 1960 to 1969 the annual real growth rate of Japan's GNP averaged 11.1 per cent, probably the highest sustained rate of increase that the world has ever seen.[16] In 1966 Japan's GNP overtook that of Italy, in 1967 that of the United Kingdom, in 1968 that of France, and in 1969 it finally surpassed that of West Germany. Japan increased its trade and payments surpluses. Since 1968 the Community has never had a surplus in its trade with Japan – indeed its deficits have been steadily growing worse.[17]

Thus, by the early 1970s, Japan had become a highly industrialized country. Even at this stage, some West European governments commented: 'A country in the course of technical modernization or industrialization is likely to benefit for a certain time from a combination of modern techniques and a low standard of living'.[18] In the late 1970s, however, Japanese wages began to approach West European levels, and by 1980 Japanese wages in the car industry were above the West European average.[19] The Commission admitted that all of this could have been predicted in 1969 and noted:

Japan would have the possibility in a few years' time of approaching, as regards volume of production and cost factor, the level of the major Western industrialized countries. . . . There are serious reasons for thinking that Japanese competitiveness at international level is more likely to improve in this new period of expansion. . . . It could be that even in the near future Japan will experience a productivity increase higher than the average, due, as in the past, to strict work discipline, to new possibilities of passing to the stage of capital-intensive production (saving rates remaining above the average), to increasingly numerous transfers of labour-intensive industries to other countries of the East and Far East.[20]

But even during the 1970s, when Japan was running on full throttle and building up capital- and technology-intensive industries, Western Europe paid little attention to it. Jean-Pierre Lehmann has compared this to the mid-1930s when West Europeans 'were ill-prepared for Japan's military onslaught'.[21]

While Japanese industry was gaining its lead in the 1970s, West European industry was already on the decline. A Commission study showed that Community industry had been labouring under cost and productivity disadvantages compared with the world's two other major trading powers, the United States and Japan.[22] During the period between the first oil crisis and 1980, the evolution of unit wage costs (in national currencies) for the manufacturing sector showed wide variations between the three: Community costs were rising by 11.2 per cent annually, the United States had an annual rise of 7.5 per cent and Japan had a rise of only 3.6 per cent. Trends in hourly productivity rates in volume terms for the same period showed the highest increase for Japan (7.2 per cent), with relatively bad performances by the United States and the Community (1.7 per cent and 3.8 per cent respectively). In the Community productivity differed widely between member states (from 1.4 per cent in the United Kingdom to 6.6 per cent in Belgium). In the period 1975-80 Japan further increased its productivity growth to 7.9 per cent, while the United States fell to 1.6 per cent and Belgium increased slightly to 6.8 per cent (see Table 12).

The Commission also analysed company accounts which revealed a weaker performance in terms of sales margins, return on assets and re-muneration of equity capital by Community companies than those of the United States and, to a lesser extent, Japan. For example, in 1980, the first hundred industrial groups in Western Europe achieved an average net profit on sales of 1.4 per cent compared with 2.4 per cent for the first hundred Japanese groups and 4.8 per cent for the first hundred US groups. The gap was also considerable in terms of net profit on capital: 6.5 per cent for West European corporations, 14 per cent for the Japanese, 15.6 per cent for the Americans.[23]

A look at the exports of manufactured products in 1980 shows that the Community was still without doubt the largest exporter in the OECD: its extra-Community exports amounted to 38.6 per cent of the OECD total, the United States taking only 22.3 per cent and Japan 19 per cent (see Table 13). However, while Japan and the United States had increased their share by 2.6 points since 1973, the Community had seen its share cut by 0.4 points. The Commission itself noted that: 'In short, were it not for the good performance of agri-industry and raw materials exports, the overall performance of the Community's exports would have been much worse. And for manufactured goods as a whole, the Community lost ground re-lative to the Japanese and the United States'.[24] The Commission was also worried that the Community as a whole remained heavily committed to exporting a wide range of medium-technology industrial products whose competitiveness was threatened both on price and on innovation.[25]

The Commission's main anxiety was that the Community was far behind both the United States and Japan in its worldwide marketing of high-technology products. The relative proportions of high-technology pro-ducts in the total exports of the three powers – the Community, the United States and Japan – showed a rapid qualitative deterioration of the Com-munity's position (see Table 14).[26] The indices show striking differences both between countries and over time: the Community fell from 1.02 in 1963 to 0.88 in 1980, compared with the United States which held rela-tively steady (from 1.29 to 1.20) and Japan which jumped from 0.56 to 1.41.

The Commission has noted that 'not only are Community exports rela-tively unspecialized, the degree of specialization in high-technology, high-skill products seems to be declining and certain member states' exports are even specializing in product areas where they are – or will be – competing mainly with newly industrializing countries, rather than with other de-veloped countries'.[27] The change in the Community's position in world-wide marketing of manufactured products, high-technology products in particular, has been accompanied by a more frequent and increasingly

Table 12 Wage costs and productivity : annual growth rates

	Unit wage costs in national currencies (%*)		Hourly productivity in volume	
	1973-80	1975-80	1973-80	1975-80
Japan	3.6	0.2	7.2	7.9
USA	7.5	7.2	1.7	1.6
EC-7	11.2	9.2	3.8	4.2
Belgium	6.1	2.9	6.6	6.8†
Denmark	7.8	6.8	4.4	3.8
France	10.0	8.7	4.9	5.1
FRG	4.7	4.2	4.8	4.2
Italy	16.0	12.4	3.5	4.9
Neth.	5.4	2.6	5.5	6.6†
UK	17.3	15.0	1.4	1.9

Source: The Commission, *The Competitiveness of the Community Industry*, Brussels, 1982, p.38.
*Calculated on the basis of logarithmic trend of index.
†1975-9.

Table 13 Changes in shares in OECD exports

	Share of OECD exports in 1980 (%)			Change 1973/1980 (% points difference)		
	Japan	USA	EC*	Japan	USA	EC
Total products	15.3	25.1	37.2	2.25	0.09	1.82
Manufactured products	19.0	22.3	38.6	2.6	0.8	−0.4

Source: The Commission, *The Competitiveness of the Community Industry* (calculations by the Commission staff on the basis of OECD trade data), Brussels 1982, p.25.
*Not including intra-Community trade.

Table 14 Index of changes in comparative advantage in exports of high-technology products

	1963	1970	1980
United States	1.29	1.27	1.20
Japan	0.56	0.87	1.41
Community (9)	1.02	0.94	0.88
Belg./Lux.	0.67	0.77	0.79
Denmark	0.58	0.60	0.66
West Germany	1.21	1.06	0.99
France	1.00	1.06	0.93
Ireland	0.43	0.67	1.03
Italy	0.84	0.83	0.63
Netherlands	1.05	0.83	0.69
United Kingdom	1.05	0.92	0.94

Source: Commission Service, DGII (Economic and Financial Affairs).

large overall deficit in the trade balance of the Community as a whole.

The success of the Japanese push into world markets owed much to its access to investment resources, enabling it to reduce its commitment to the technologically less advanced sectors and move on to the more specialized sectors, knowing that any short-term losses would be offset by future long-term gains.

The West European countries did not take due account of developments in Japan and were unable to reduce their dependence on traditional in-

Table 15 Investment in manufacturing (1975 prices and exchange rates)

	Community			Japan			USA		
	1970	1975	1979	1970	1975	1979	1970	1975	1979
Total investment									
1000 mECU	229	236	263	111	131	170	202	201	255
% of GDP	24	22	21	35	32	33	18	16	17
Manufacturing investment 1000 mECU									
(approx.)	53	42	39	30	25	27	26	26	36
% of GDP	5.2	3.8	3.0	9.6	6.1	5.2	2.8	2.1	2.6
% of total investment	23	18	15	27	19	16	13	13	14

Source: USA – national accounts, EBA aggregates; Japan – Economic Planning Agency; Community – Eurostat.

dustrial sectors such as steel, shipbuilding and parts of the chemical industry. So they were outstripped by Japan and the United States in investments in the technologically specialized sectors.[28]

Defensive European responses

West European industry reacted to the success of the Japanese either by urging restraint on the part of the exporters or by putting barriers in their way. Early in the 1980s, agreements were already being reached between Community industries and their counterparts in third countries defining appropriate market shares: the understanding between motor industries in the United Kingdom and Japan was a case in point. There were more institutionalized restrictions in other areas. The Community itself maintained a panoply of bilaterally negotiated controls on steel imports from sources ranging from Eastern Europe to South Korea, while seeking to have minimum price levels maintained within the Community. Textiles producers in the Community pushed member governments into adopting a rigid stand on imports from developing countries in the talks on a new international MFA to replace agreements in place since 1973. The restrictions were intended to buy time for industrial adjustment, to enable industries to adapt so as to cope with cheap imports.[29] However, critics of such policies had consistently argued that restrictions, in whatever form, were an impediment to adjustment and change.[30]

Such a position of declining competitiveness for Western Europe in relation to Japan and the United States could perhaps also be attributed to serious differences between member states and the consequent fragmentation of Community policy. These factors made it difficult for the Commission to control the commercial or self-restraint agreements between governments or industries of the member states and their Japanese counterparts. Consequently the EC failed to implement its common commercial policy, thus perpetrating an incoherent approach to Japan.

On 14 November 1962 the Council decided, on the basis of a Commission proposal, that a common safeguard clause should be included in all bilateral trade agreements with Japan. In February 1963 the Commission asked all member governments to inform the Japanese officially of this decision although it had not yet been put into practice.[31] Then on 30 April 1963, the Benelux countries signed a protocol amending the trade agreement with Japan to include a bilateral safeguard clause, and on 14 May 1963, France signed a trade agreement with Japan including a similar safeguard clause.[32]

In September 1970 the Community and Japan began official negotiations on a common trade agreement. But during exploratory negotiations France and the Benelux countries had already made it clear to the Commission that they would prefer to maintain their safeguard clauses with Japan than have a joint Community agreement with it.

As discussed in Chapter 2, from 1972 to 1974 and again in 1981 there had been fierce confrontations between the Commission (or the Community) and some member states over the voluntary restraint agreements concluded between them individually and Japan. There had also been conflicts between the Commission and France over Japanese cars being held up in French ports (in 1980) and Japanese VTRs in a tiny French customs office (in 1982).

Under these circumstances, the Japanese felt it was neither necessary nor advantageous to negotiate with the Community as a whole, that is with the Commission as its representative. A typical perception by a member of Japanese cabinet at that time was:

For Japan, the relationship with the United States is much more important. The Community is one large organization with which we have a relationship. But basically that amounts to a series of bilateral relationships between Japan and West Germany, the United Kingdom, France, etc. We feel, therefore, we should address problems in a bilateral manner.[33]

By the early 1980s, the Commission had begun to find its relationship with Japan humiliating and frustrating. In a statement of its point of view, it observed that 'the Community's trade agreements with regard to Japan are embodied in a patchwork of separate national trade restrictions which are more a relic of the 1950s than a Community policy for the 1980s'.[34] It enumerated the following examples:

(1) Certain member states (United Kingdom, France and the Benelux countries) have bilateral safeguard clauses derived from past trade agreements with Japan.

(2) Italy has a right of derogation for a number of items which have been liberalized with regard to Japan.

(3) Most member states also maintain residual QRs on Japanese goods, also derived from past bilateral agreements. Some of these restrictions are applied selectively to a number of countries including Japan but not to other major industrialized trading partners; a few discriminate against Japan alone.

(4) There are a number of informal arrangements restricting imports from Japan, negotiated annually at national level, notably by certain industries.

The Commission stressed that such a situation was unsatisfactory on a number of grounds.

First, the trade restrictions were discrimination and a source of growing resentment in Japan, quite disproprotionate to their economic importance. Second, they represented a gap in Community commercial policy, there being no unified policy in relation to QRs, and voluntary restraint arrangements of equal or greater importance being negotiated on a. separate national basis. Such bilateral negotiations meant that third countries could play member states off against each other: this squandered the collective strength of the Community and made the defence of its interests less effective. Finally, differences in the way member states treated imports from Japan were bound to lead to a distortion of conditions of competition within the Community and to a partitioning of national markets. This would damage the prosperity of large sectors of Community industry in the 1990s.

As has been made clear, some EC member states were making strong demands for intervention – countries with old protectionist habits and national jealousies who were guided by narrow national interests or prejudices about Japan. For example, France had never had much interest in trade with Japan. In 1956 Japan was interested in imports of Alsatian potash, nickel from New Caledonia and Moroccan phosphates, but France only wanted to sell perfumes, wines and cars.[35] For more than thirty years France allowed little possibility for its exports to Japan to expand.

Meanwhile, like some other member states, France had always been afraid of Japanese competition in its colonial markets, and had continued to protect its industry. The connections between some member states and their former colonies were developed under the Lomé Convention, which now includes 66 developing countries in a preferential trading arrangement.

In June 1960, even *Le Monde* described France as more protectionist towards Japan than vice versa.[36] In the early 1960s, in its trade with Japan, France in fact imported less than half as much as it exported.[37] In 1962, a senior official of the French government pointed out that it had exported less to Japan than to West Germany, Italy, the United Kingdom, the Netherlands and even Switzerland. It admitted that 'France has neglected the Japanese market'.[38] The French attitude to Japan, however, remained more or less unchanged, even though since 1962 contacts between industries, and since 1967 regular consultations between senior government officials of the two countries, had taken place. The French position was also said to have been partly a result of its bowing to stiff industrial pressure, initially mainly from the textile industry, then from the motor industry (from Renault and Peugeot, for example) and the electronics industry (e.g. Thomson-Brandt).[39]

For example, Renault repeatedly called for a more aggressively protectionist policy to hold back Japanese car exports to West European markets.[40] Thomson-Brandt, one of the oligopolistic European-based electronics manufacturers, has consistently and efficiently lobbied together with Philips to restrain Japanese exports.[41]

One of the most typical examples of consistent industrial pressure, however, was from Philips in the Benelux countries. In March 1972, when a Benelux electronics industry delegation visited Japan to ask for a VER agreement on Japanese electronics exports to the Benelux countries the Dutch government, reportedly at the suggestion of Philips, threatened to apply their bilateral safeguard clauses against Japan.[42] In August 1972, when the Dutch government repeated its threat, Philips's pressure was once again discernible.[43]

Then, in 1977, when Hitachi, one of the Japanese electronics giants, revealed its plan to set up a plant in the United Kingdom, the most active opponent was again a Philips subsidiary, Mullard.[44] In April 1980, Philips asked the Community to introduce a quota system for Japanese television imports in line with the United States, and threatened publicly that otherwise it could only conclude there was no point in continuing in Europe.[45]

Finally, in 1983, when the export restraint agreement on Japanese VTRs was concluded between the Community and Japan, *The Financial Times* explicitly stated that one of its main purposes was 'to protect Europe's indigenous video recorder industry, Philips and Grundig'.[46]

Italian industry has also been conspicuously protectionist. In 1973 when Honda Motor told the Italian government it wanted to set up an assembly plant for lightweight motor cycles in Italy, Fiat and Moto Guzzi lobbied strongly to prevent this new competition, and Guzzi threatened that if Honda was allowed in, Guzzi would pull out its production.[47]

The Commission's inability to win a clear mandate to negotiate with Japan was due not only to the factors already mentioned, but also the wide divergence of trade policy traditions between the member states – some with strong protectionist habits and others with a free trade orientation. Thus the character of the Community created difficulties for third countries. Individual member states have, in practice, kept a substantial amount of control over external trade, though the Treaty of Rome gives the Commission considerable authority on this matter. Third countries have been confused about the respective roles of the Commission and the member states – a source of friction between the Community and third countries which continues. Gardner Patterson indicated that the Japanese had long been somewhat bewildered by the Community, and gave an example as follows:

No less a person than the chief Japanese negotiator during the latter stages of the Tokyo round drew strong protests from the Commission for expressing publicly some doubts and concerns over the respective negotiating roles of the member states and the Commission.[48]

According to Patterson, an important reason why the Japanese have a strong reason for dealing directly with member states is that the Community does not in fact have an all-inclusive common commercial policy, as they are subject to a series of discriminatory import restrictions applied by certain of the member states, though not by all.

Regarding the Community's competence in its external relations, Article 210 of the Treaty provides that the 'Community shall have legal personality'. In July 1964, however, the European Court of Justice gave its Opinion (6/64) that this Community's international personality, which is reflected in the Community's capacity or competence to act in international relations, derives from a limitation of sovereignty or a transfer of powers from the member states to the Community.[49] In March 1971 the Court gave another Opinion (22/70) that 'this provision means that in its external relations the Community enjoys the capacity to establish contractual links with third countries over the whole field of objectives defined in Part One of the Treaty'.[50] Member states which are the constituent parts of the Community are, therefore, represented by the Commission where EC competence is established, and in most cases this competence is exclusive, in the sense that the transfer of powers to the Community precludes the member states from acting concurrently or so as to impede Community action.[51]

Concerning the Community's jurisdiction over commercial policy, Article 3 of the Treaty states that a common commercial policy towards third countries is to be established, and Articles 110-116 deal with the implementation of this policy provided that member states 'shall co-ordinate their trade relations with third countries' during the original transition period (Article 111), and after this period has ended, 'the common commercial policy shall be based on uniform principles, particularly in regard to changes in tariff rates . . .' (Article 113).

Article 113 provides the basis for a common commercial policy. It identifies five areas as relevant: (1) changes in tariff rates; (2) the conclusion of tariff and trade agreements; (3) the achievement of uniformity in measures of liberalization; (4) export policy; and (5) measures to protect trade such as those to be taken in cases of dumping or subsidies. It avoids an exhaustive enumeration of EC competence.

EC commercial policy does not rest solely on commercial criteria, but can involve general economic and some political considerations. The Community tends, therefore, to go beyond the limits of the powers provided in Article 113, and member countries having liberal bilateral relations have to be treated as concerned parties on those commercial policy issues that are under the Community's jurisdiction. In these circumstances, commercial policy has to be administered through a composite or mixed procedure involving both the Community and member states.[52] This bred confusion as to the Community's jurisdiction and caused a lot of problems: complicating and delaying negotiations, perplexing non-member countries and making them distrustful of the Community's international status.

Despite attempts at clarification once the transitional period of the Treaty of Rome was completed, the intended scope or content of a common commercial policy in the Community remained confusing and controversial.[53] In the early 1970s, therfore, it was stressed repeatedly, even by the Commission, that Article 113 was hardly a basis for a meaningful common commercial policy,[54] and in May 1970 the European Parliament emphasized in a decision that 'the Community must make progress particularly in the field of harmonization of the national policies on the modern aspects of trading relations with non-member countries'. The Court of Justice in expressing its Opinions on the issues raised by the Commission under Article 228 of the Treaty, had to work to clarify the situation.

The Court produced, in the second half of 1970s, two important Opinions on the Community's jurisdiction in the field of external trade. First, in November 1975 the Court stated in its Opinion 1/75 that the Community has exclusive powers to implement the uniform principles provided in Article 113.[55] The current situation is, however, set forth in the Court Opinion 1/78, which holds that the Community has the legal powers needed to conduct coherent commercial policy. It states that:

Although it may be thought that at the time when the Treaty was drafted liberalization of trade was the dominant idea, the Treaty nevertheless does not form a barrier to the possibility of the Community's developing a commercial policy aiming at a regulation of the world market for certain products rather than at a mere liberalization of trade.

Article 113 empowers the Community to formulate a commercial 'policy', based on 'uniform principles' thus showing that the question of external trade must be governed from a wide point of view and not only having regard to the administration of precise systems such as customs and quantitative restrictions. The same conclusion may be deduced from the fact that the enumeration in·Article 113 of the subjects covered by commercial policy is conceived as a non-exhaustive enumeration which must not, as such, close the door to the application in a Community context of any other process intended to regulate external trade. A restrictive interpretation of the concept of common commercial policy would risk causing disturbances which would then exist in certain sectors of economic relations with non-member countries.[56]

The common commercial policy has now moved beyond the transitional period but it is still incomplete, because the Community cannot yet enjoy the sole powers it is eventually intended to have. Policies still vary from one EC member state to another, covering the range from the more liberal to the more protectionist. The situation is far from satisfactory.

4 Agenda for Adjustment

Structural reforms in Japan

In the light of the persistent frustration and complaints over Japan's long-lasting, huge trade surplus with the Community in particular, and some stereotyped anecdotes claiming that it was still keeping its market closed, the Japanese government has taken a series of measures to reduce NTBs and promote imports throughout the 1970s and 1980s. Since the mid-1980s in particular, it has strengthened these efforts and implemented a number of market-opening measures, including the Action Program of 1985 for improved market access and the ¥6 trillion budget package of 1987. These affected tariffs, administrative barriers, technical safety regulations, testing requirements, taxation changes and public expenditure, and were designed to reduce dependence on exports and promote an economy led by domestic demand.

As a result, Japan now has the lowest tariffs and perhaps the lowest NTBs among the major industrialized countries, although NTBs other than QRs are difficult to identify and compare internationally.[1] At any rate, Japan is 'at the end of the spectrum in terms of formal NTBs and their effects on trade'.[2]

The average tariff on industrial products entering Japan has for some years been lower than those applying in the United States and the Community. In 1987, when the tariff reductions agreed in the Tokyo round were completed, Japan's average rate was only 3 per cent, lower than that of either the United States (4.2 per cent) or the Community (4.9 per cent).[3]

Even after the Tokyo round, Japan continued to reduce or eliminate tariffs on its own initiative. On the basis of the Action Program, the government has slashed tariffs still further to encourage imports:

- In 1986 – on 1 January, tariffs on 1,849 items were either eliminated or reduced by an average of 20 per cent; on 20 January, tariffs on nine electronics items were removed; and on 1 April, tariffs on four items such as bottled wine were reduced by 20 per cent (and were further lowered in 1987).[4]

Table 16

(a) Tariff burden of selected industrialized countries and the Community, 1987

Japan	Community	United States	Canada
2.6%	2.7%	3.6%	4.3%

Source: Japanese Ministry of Finance.
Note: The tariff burden is the ratio of tariff revenue to total import value. The figure for the Community does not include import surcharges on agricultural products.

(b) Examples of tariff reduction or elimination (%)

	1979	1980	1981	1982	1983	1984	1985	1986
Semiconductors	12.0	—	—	4.2	—	—	0	—
Computers	—	—	9.1	7.0	4.9	—	—	0
Tyres & tyre cases	—	—	—	—	—	—	4.0	0
Skis & parts	—	—	—	—	—	—	6.0	4.8
Palm oil	—	—	—	—	4.0*	3.0*	0*	—
Batik	—	—	—	—	—	—	—†	0*

Source: Japanese Ministry of Finance.
* = GSP. † = Not GSP.
Note: A dash means not available; zero means close to zero.

- In 1987 – on 1 April, tariffs on 33 products with tariff concession rates of 2 per cent or less were eliminated and tariffs on 10 forest products were reduced; in April, by improvements of the Generalized System of Preferences (GSP), the ceiling on zero preferential tariffs for almost half the industrial products was eliminated and the ceiling for most remaining products was raised by an average of 30 per cent; and in fiscal year (FY) 1987, tariffs on cigarettes and alcoholic beverages were reduced.

As for residual QRs, the Japanese government has reduced these restrictions considerably since the early 1960s. As a result, the number of items under these restrictions decreased from 466 in March 1962 to 23 in April 1986. Among these 23 items, only one is a mining and manufacturing product (coal). It should therefore be clear that the removal of these restrictions on mining and manufacturing products is practically completed.

Though residual QRs still remain on 22 agricultural products such as

Table 17 The process of import liberalization in Japan, 1960-86
Positive list

Year	Month	Liberalization	
		Ratio (%)	Number of Items
1960	4	41	1443
	7	42	1504
	10	44	1985
1961	4	62	2645
	7	65	2757
	10	68	3257
	12	70	3427

Negative list

Year	Month	Residual import restrictions			Total number of items under import restrictions
		Total	Manufactures & minerals	Agricultural & fisheries prod.	
1962	4	466	—	—	492
	10	232	—	—	292
1963	4	197	—	—	229
	8	155	87	68	192
1964	1	152	84	68	189
	4	136	69	67	174
	5	136	69	67	174
	10	123	56	67	162
1965	10	122	55	67	161
1966	4	120	54	66	159
1968	4	122	54	68	165
1969	4	120	52	68	163
	10	118	50	68	161
1970	2	109	45	64	152
	4	98	39	59	141
1971	1	80	31	49	123
	6	60	20	40	106
	10	40	12	28	87
1972	4	33	9	24	79
1973	4	32	8	24	83
	11	31	8	23	82
1974	10	30	8	22	84
	12	29	7	22	83

Table 17, negative list, ctd.

Year	Month	Total	Manufactures & minerals	Agricultural & fisheries prod	Total number of items under import restrictions
		Residual import restrictions			
1975	4	29	7	22	84
	12	27	5	22	82
1977	4	27	5	22	80
1978	4	27	5	22	79
1980	1	27	5	22	73
	5	27	5	22	84
1981	10	27	5	22	79
1982	3	27	5	22	79
1984	5	27	5	22	80
	7	27	5	22	80
1985	4	27	5	22	80
1986	4	23	1	22	76

Source: Japanese Ministry of Finance.

beef and citrus fruits, the restrictions will be eliminated in FY 1992; and of the ten agricultural products which Japan has been called on to bring into line with the GATT, eight are to be liberalized by 1 April 1990.[5]

The Action Program also called for a review of 91 points in connection with the improvement of standards, certification systems and import procedures; almost all of these were completed as scheduled by the end of July 1988. As a result, import procedures for automobiles, cosmetics, electrical appliances, medical equipment, telecommunications equipment and other products have become much easier and faster.[6] Follow-up action is in progress with the establishment of mechanisms for switching from government certification to self-certification, and the formulation of guidelines for foreign participation in various councils, the definition of standard time limits for the completion of certification procedures, and the acceptance of foreign test data.

With regard to automobiles, the Japanese government has abolished the requirement on the submission of durability test data, shortened type approval procedure to only two months (compared with nine months in West Germany and six-and-a-half months for exhaust emission control tests in the United States), and strengthened the system of sending Japanese officials overseas to test automobiles for type approval at the place of manufacture.

That these measures have been effective can be seen in the fact that the value of automobile imports into Japan in 1986 totalled $1.13 billion on a

Table 18 QRs eliminated by the Japanese government in 1988

Effective date	
October 1988	Fruit puree and paste (non-citrus)
	Fruit pulp (apple, grape and peach)
	Baby food, juice
	Lentils, chickpeas
April 1989	Processed cheese
	Non-citrus fruit juices other than apple, grape or pineapple
July 1989	Tomato juice
	Tomato ketchup and sauce
Oct. 1988–	Whipped cream in pressurized containers; high-value-added
April 1990	dairy products such as frozen yoghurt and ice cream; pasta
	Beef and pork prepared products
April 1990	Certain sugar and sugar liquids
	Fruit puree and paste (citrus)
	Fruit pulp (citrus)
	Prepared and preserved pineapple
	Apple, grape and pineapple juice
	Prepared products made mainly from sugar
	Beef
	Oranges, fresh
	Oranges, temporarily chilled
	Orange juice

Source: Japanese Ministry of Agriculture, Forestry and Fishery.

customs clearance basis (a 97 per cent rise over the previous year) and $2.11 billion in 1987 (an 87 per cent increase from 1986). Registration of imported vehicles hit a new record of 68,357 units in 1986, a 36.2 per cent increase over the previous year. In 1987 the figure was 97,750 units, a 42.9 per cent increase. Of these, vehicles imported from Western Europe amounted to 94,524 units in 1987, a 41.9 per cent increase over 1986.[7]

In the Action Program, the Japanese government decided to improve contract procedures substantially and to expand the purchase of foreign products. The government and its related organizations began to use competitive tendering more extensively. The proportion of contracts awarded on the basis of competitive tendering rose from 66 per cent in terms of value in 1984 to 81 per cent in 1986 and 1987. This figure compares favourably with 65 per cent in the Community. In terms of the number of contracts, the ratio rose to 91 per cent in 1987 from 69 per cent in 1984.[8]

The procurement of foreign goods by the designated 67 entities in 1987 increased by 26 per cent to ¥54.8 billion, more than in 1986, and the num-

Table 19 Comparison of residual QRs

Country	Agricultural & fisheries products		Manufactures & minerals		Total	
	(1)	(2)	(1)	(2)	(1)	(2)
Japan	55	22	35	1	90	23
United States	1	1	4	6	5	7
West Germany	19	3	20	1	39	4
United Kingdom	19	1	6	2	25	3
France	39	19	35	27	74	46
Italy	12	3	8	5	20	8
Benelux	10	2	4	3	14	5
Denmark	62	5	2	0	64	5

Source: GATT.
Notes: (1) At the end of December 1979, (2) At the end of April 1987.

ber of foreign procurement contracts rose to 1,925, up by 72 per cent on the previous year. The Community increased its share in numbers as well as value in the procurement of contracts with the Japanese government and its related organizations. Procurement from the Community increased by ¥9.2 billion, or 200 per cent from 1986 to 1987 – more than the ¥8 billion, or 43 per cent, from the United States. As a result, the ratio of foreign pro-ducts in Japan's total designated procurement has marked 13 per cent since 1985, in comparison with the figure of 12.2 per cent for the United States and 2.1 per cent for the Community (according to official Japanese sources).[9]

During these few years, Japan allowed the British Cable and Wireless to participate in the operation of Japan's international telecommunications business; foreign securities companies were given membership of the Tokyo Stock Exchange; the liquor tax was amended to reduce the internal tax on Scotch whisky; Japan took steps to reduce its local automobile tax which, according to the Commission, was disadvantageous for Community cars of more than 2,000 cc; and Japan has decided to purchase a number of high-unit price Community products, for example three Super Pumas produced by Aerospatiale of France, a number of Airbus aircraft worth ¥160 billion, and Falcon-900s produced by Dassault-Breguet of France (a deal worth ¥10 billion).[10]

Japan is poorly endowed with natural resources and land, and has to import almost all the important items such a crude oil, other fuels, other raw materials and food. Hence the trade pattern has been one of importing raw materials and exporting manufactured products. Furthermore, given the absence so far of advanced industrial economies in the region, Japan has tended to produce the necessary industrial products domestically.

However, since the early 1980s, Japan's imports of manufactured goods have grown faster than those of any other industrial nation. Japan has instituted far-reaching measures to promote these imports. Community exports of manufactured products to Japan have increased faster than those from the United States or the world as a whole in the past few years. In 1986 and 1987, for example, while the United States expanded its exports of manufactured goods to Japan by 23.9 and 0.2 per cent, Community exports of manufactured goods jumped by 55.5 and 26.7 per cent, albeit from a low base (see Table 20).

It becomes apparent that Japan's imports from the Community have been steadily increasing since 1986. The rate of increase has been greater than that for Japan's exports to the Community. In 1988, for example, Japan's imports from the Community increased by 36.2 per cent compared with the previous year in dollar terms, whereas Japan's exports to the Community increased by only 24.3 per cent. As a result, the rate of increase of Japan's trade surplus with the Community fell from 45.1 per cent in 1986 to 20 per cent in 1987 and 13.9 per cent in 1988 in dollar terms. Moreover, when calculated in yen, the rate of increase was only 3.5 per cent in 1986 and 1987, and the surplus decreased slightly, by 0.1 per cent in 1988 (see Table 21).

It should also be pointed out that Japan is rapidly expanding its direct investment in the Community in preparation for the single European market.[11] Japanese firms expect that 1992 will open considerable opportunities for them if they have the advantage of actually operating from within the world's largest market of 320 million customers. They are also worried that the single market might become less accessible to foreign trading partners, although the Community has committed itself to seeing that this is not the case.

While the Community and some member states with protectionist tendencies have expressed unhappiness over so-called 'screwdriver' assembly plants, the Community has been generally receptive to Japanese direct investment, which could result in both greater employment and technology transfer, and consequently could contribute to the revitalization of the Community's economy.

Until the middle of 1987, the Community criticized Japan over its problems of access to the Japanese market and over the continuation of allegedly irresponsible mercantilist policies by the Japanese government. In a statement in March 1987, the Council deplored the continuing deterioration of its trade deficit with Japan. It blamed the Japanese for the failure to reach a so-called 'balance of benefits'.[12]

However, as it became clear that Japan's trade surplus with the Community was beginning to stabilize, the Community's tone gradually changed. In April 1988, the Council adopted a conclusion which actually

Table 20 Japan's imports of manufactured goods

	1986	1987
Value of manufactured imports ($m)		
Total	52,781	65,961
United States	17,645	17,672
Community	11,956	15,145
Rate of increase (%)		
Total	31.4	25.0
United States	23.9	0.2
Community	55.5	26.7
Value of imports ($m)		
Total	126,408	149,515
United States	29,054	31,490
Community	13,989	17,670
Manufactured imports as share of total (%)		
Total	41.8	44.1
United States	60.7	56.1
Community	85.5	85.7

Source: Boeki tokei (Trade Statistics), Japanese Ministry of Finance.

Table 21 Trade between Japan and the Community (¥ bn, $m)

	Balance		Japanese exports		Japanese imports	
Year	Yen	Dollar	Yen	Dollar	Yen	Dollar
1986	2825	18,686	5174	30,675	2348	13,989
1987	2923	20,024	5488	37,693	2565	17,670
1988	2919	22,798	6002	46,867	3083	24,069
Changes from previous year						
1986	+3.5	+45.1	+4.5	+47.5	+5.6	+50.5
1987	+3.5	+20.0	+6.1	+22.9	+9.2	+26.3
1988	−0.1	+13.9	+9.4	+24.3	+20.2	+36.2

Source: Customs Statistics, Japanese Ministry of Finance.
Note: Comparison with 1985 figures is calculated on a 12-member-state basis.

welcomed the Japanese government's 'commitment to structural reforms' and economic growth, and confirmed that 'things are moving in the right direction'.[13] Nevertheless, Hans-Dietrich Genscher, the West German Foreign Minister, noted after the Council had adopted this conclusion, 'the lack of balance in Euro-Japanese trade is still a serious problem'.[14]

In the past few years there has been another striking phenomenon. Japan's trade with the Community has developed differently from that with the world as a whole. As might be expected from the movement of exchange rates, Japan's exports to the Community have grown steadily, while those to the world as a whole and to the United States have fallen. As a result, Japan's trade surplus with the Community on the basis of yen has increased by 3.5 per cent in 1986, 3.5 per cent in 1987, and remained almost stable (decrease of 0.1 per cent) in 1988, though its surplus with the world as a whole and the United States dropped considerably. With the United States, it fell by 7.7 per cent, 12.5 per cent and 19.4 per cent.

These trends have created serious problems with the Community, which has had little scope for establishing a balance between the two parties. For example, it has been difficult for Community exporters of manufactured goods to convince anyone that visible import barriers, such as tariffs or QRs, were what prevented them from exporting to Japan. The Community's complaints, therefore, began to converge on 'the habits and attitudes bred of Japan's vertically and horizontally integrated industrial, commercial and financial groups'.[15] At the same time, the Community has also strengthened some of its protective devices by maintaining QRs against products imported from Japan, applying strict rules on Community content, establishing new anti-dumping rules (the 'screwdriver' regulation), and planning to introduce 'reciprocity' criteria in financial services.

Many of the relevant sectors are not yet covered by the GATT but will be included in the 1992 programme. In the Uruguay round, however, efforts are now being made to extend GATT to fields such as services, investments and intellectual property rights, some of which are also covered by the 1992 programme. The Community indicated that even after 1992 it may maintain QRs for some sensitive products such as cars, but as a Community-wide measure.

The rest of Chapter 4 and Chapter 5 will comment on various aspects of integration and related issues, notably QRs and the automobile sector which, though not essential to the process, are crucial to trade relations between Japan and the Community. Other areas of study include Japan's direct investment in the Community and related matters, new anti-dumping regulations, local content requirements and rules of origin; and the concept of reciprocity.

Table 22 Discriminatory QRs on imports from Japan, 1 December 1988

Country	Agri-cultural	Industrial	Total	Applied only to Japan
Benelux	0	7	7	7
West Germany	0	2	2	2
Denmark	0	2	2	2
France	4	13	17	5
United Kingdom	0	0	0	0
Greece	0	2	2	0
Italy	3	33	36	33
Ireland	0	1	1	0
Spain	1	40	41	41
Portugal	0	23	23	23
Total Community	8	123	131	113

Sources: OJ C37, 16 February 1987; OJ C57, 5 March 1987; and Japanese Ministry of Foreign Affairs.
Note: Discriminatory QRs applied to the state trading countries are not taken.

Quantitative restrictions – discrimination

More than thirty years after the signing of the Treaty of Rome, the Community still has no common commercial policy towards Japan. Instead, many member states have maintained national QRs on imports from Japan (see Table 22). As of December 1988, a total of 131 nationally imposed restrictions on 107 products are being applied against Japan, although the United Kingdom totally eliminated them by the end of 1967. The Community accession agreements allowed certain member states to keep some of their residual QRs, most of which had derived from bilateral treaties previously agreed with Japan. For example, Italy maintains the most rigid import restrictions on cars from Japan, with an annual limit of 2,550 cars and 750 off-road vehicles for 1989.

In the Community's trade relations with the world as a whole, over 1,000 products are currently covered by national QRs (the majority directed at imports from state trading countries). The member states with the most extensive list of national QRs are Italy, France and Spain. Most of the QRs are on textiles and, in the case of Spain, also on a wider range of agricultural and industrial products. For Japanese products, Spain has 41 and Italy 36 discriminatory restrictions.

Under Community law, these national measures against Japan are legal. With the transitional period over, member states cannot in principle maintain national commercial measures without the Community's special permission, but the common rules for imports No. 288/82 permit national QRs against third countries in certain circumstances.[16] According to Article 1 of Regulation No. 288/82, importation into the Community of products originating from third countries is, with some exceptions, free and not subject to QRs; but QRs for 'products listed in Annexe 1' (negative lists) are legalized 'without prejudice' to their maintenance.[17] Therefore, member states may impose national QRs against Japan under Community regulations provided that the products concerned are listed in Annexe 1.

In the first half of the 1960s, the United Kingdom, France and the Benelux countries concluded bilateral trade agreements with Japan on the MFN basis. They signed trade protocols which contained both renewal safeguard clauses and negative lists of products on which existing QRs would be maintained. These bilateral trade agreements were provisional, and new Community-based agreements should have been concluded after the transitional period, i.e. from January 1970, under Article 113 (3) of the Treaty.

But after the transitional period, member states maintained their bilateral agreements with third countries (apart from state trading countries), and efforts to conclude a common trade agreement with Japan reached deadlock. In 1969, the Council decided to allow member states to renew existing agreements with third countries provided they did not contain any obstacles to the realization of the common commercial policy.[18] Since then, the various agreements between member states and Japan have been renewed regularly.

However, these national measures against Japan are clearly incompatible with the provisions of the GATT in two ways: not only are they QRs, but they are discriminatory restrictions imposed against Japan and other third countries. They are also incompatible with the roll-back commitment made by contracting parties in the Punta del Este Declaration.

The GATT provides for the general elimination of QRs (Article 11) and non-discriminatory administration of these restrictions (Article 13) to achieve its objectives of the substantial reduction or elimination of trade barriers and non-discriminatory treatment in international trade. Article 11 (1) prescribes that:

No prohibitions or restrictions other than duties, taxes or other charges, whether made effective through quotas, import or export licences or other measures, shall be instituted or maintained by any contracting party on the importation of any product of the territory of any other contracting party or on the exportation or sale for export of any product destined for the territory of any other contracting party.

By this provision, all contracting parties are prohibited from instituting or maintaining any trade barriers, QRs in particular, other than duties, taxes or other charges, on imports from other contracting parties. Contracting parties, however, do not necessarily have to eliminate all QRs and may maintain some restrictions, for example to safeguard domestic agricultural and fisheries products[19] and the balance of payments.[20] Other clauses provide for general exceptions[21] and security exceptions.[22]

However, QRs which are permitted under these terms have to be applied indiscriminately to all contracting parties in accordance with Article 13 (1) which provides that:

No prohibition or restriction shall be applied by any contracting party on the importation of any product of the territory of any other contracting party or on the exportation of any product destined for the territory of any other contracting party, unless the importation of the like product of all third countries or the exportation of the like product to all third countries is similarly prohibited or restricted.

In addition, most of these QRs are perceived in Japan as arbitrary because they do not appear necessary from an economic point of view. The items subject to discriminatory QRs are not always sensitive for the member states. In practice, for many items, the actual volume of imports from Japan far exceeds the limit established in the QRs. For other items, imports from Japan fall far below the limit set in the restrictions and would remain well below it even in the absence of any restriction. In the first case, limitation is not enforced; in the second, the level of imports would not exceed the limit anyway. Thus it is difficult to find a real economic rationale for their existence. A senior official of the Japanese government said, 'These restrictions are what may be termed "relics from a former age" – namely, an age when Japan was a low-wage country'.[23]

The Community sometimes uses a curious logic. The Commission said that: 'There is no evidence that the Community's QRs have substantially reduced Japanese export possibilities. Japan's exports to Europe . . . have grown at the fastest pace imaginable. This means that, even if there had been no QRs in certain sectors such as automobiles or TV and radio equipment, Japanese exports would not have gown faster. Other defence mechanisms, such as self-restraint agreements, would have been triggered'.[24]

Of a total of 131 discriminatory QRs, 113 are applied only to Japan, and the remaining 18 to Japan and other countries. It is not surprising that Japan should find this politically unacceptable. Furthermore, that the Community, the world's largest trading entity of advanced industrial countries, should maintain so many discriminatory QRs on imports from Japan jeopardizes the future of the Community-Japan partnership and free trade in general.

These discriminatory national restrictions on imports from Japan imply a loophole or unnecessary anomaly in the Community's regulations. They are a deviation from the uniform principles for a common commercial policy provided in Article 113 of the Treaty. They are also logically incompatible with the concept of an integrated market, the Community objective for 1992.

Japan has of course made strong and repeated demands to the Community for the immediate elimination of these restrictions. In July 1980, while the Commission noted that some of the residual QRs against Japanese products 'are on goods which are important in trade', it admitted that 'many of them are anachronistic or of little obvious value'.[25] In addition, the Commission pointed out that the need to develop cooperation with Japan was being hindered by the maintenance of national protectionist measures such as QRs, and stressed that 'there should be a political willingness to start phasing out the discriminatory QRs'.[26]

Following several discussions on this matter with the Japanese government, the Commission has itself been tackling these anomalies. In March 1989, the Commission notified Japan that it would lift 42 of 131 QRs on products imported from Japan.[27] But this is only a small portion of the total, and excludes such major Japanese export items as cars, motor cycles and electrical household appliances.[28] It seems unlikely, therefore, to have any major impact on overall Japanese exports to the Community.

As part of its 1992 programme, the Community envisages eliminating border controls between member states so as to ensure the free movement of people and goods. It will then become physically impossible for state authorities to enforce national QRs with third countries. This should logically lead to the liberalization of more areas of the Community trade regime.

On 19 October 1988, after the Commission had concluded its debate on the external dimension of the 1992 single market, it issued an information memo stating that:

The establishment of the internal market will result in the removal of the remaining disparities in import and export arrangements. At present there are certain quantitative restrictions in the member states of the Community affecting mainly East European countries and Japan and also involving the national quotas under the textile agreements or GSP. Completion of the single market will mean the removal of QRs and will require unified import rules in respect of non-Community countries.[29]

But the memo also suggested that continued protection may be required in certain sensitive sectors and some of the existing national QRs may be transformed into Community-wide protective measures:

It is possible, however, that in a number of sensitive spheres, national measures will have to be replaced by Community measures. If this proves to be the case, the Community will adopt these measures in line with its international obligations and following discussions with its partners. These measures would not result in a higher level of protection than exists as present.

Japan finds this paragraph particularly disturbing, since it raises the possibility of discriminatory QRs being transformed into restrictions at the Community level.

The United States has also criticized the Community's policy on this matter. Peter McPherson, then Deputy Secretary of the Treasury, warned that if current national QRs on certain imported goods were not abolished but were instead transformed into Community-wide barriers, they could hurt US exports and also result in goods now exported to Western Europe being diverted to the United States. He added that 'this would harm our efforts to reduce the trade deficit'.[30] The United States also issued a document pointing out that 'Community goals related to the completion of the internal market do not justify transformation of the existing national QRs into Community-wide barriers. The United States objects to any continuation of these import restraints even on a "transitional" basis'. It stressed that 'sectors facing actual or threatened injury from import competition should have their case examined in accordance with the GATT rules under Article 19 (or a potential new safeguard agreement)'.[31]

The United States government considers that product areas where the Community may be contemplating Community-wide protective measures include: automobiles, footwear, urea, consumer electronics and bananas, and that trade restrictions might also be under consideration for sewing machines, motor cycles, dishware and certain ceramic articles.[32]

One possibility might be for the Community to transform some national QRs benefiting particular countries like Italy and France into VER agreements on products such as automobiles between the Community as a whole and Japan or other newly industrialized countries.

The United States was also afraid that wide-ranging repercussions on its interests might result if QRs are turned into Community-wide grey-area measures such as VER agreements.[33] It pointed out that Japan might try to circumvent a Community-Japan VER agreement on automobiles by shifting production to the United States; meanwhile, trends in the Community were moving towards setting local content requirements to prevent this type of invasion.

Will the Community maintain discriminatory restrictions against Japan after 1992? This is a crucial question in judging whether it is really determined to maintain a liberal and open external trade system, as its top officials have repeatedly claimed.

Automobiles – a sensitive sector

In Western Europe, most of the major car-producing countries protect themselves against Japanese imports.

Italy has maintained the most rigorous quota on the importation of Japanese cars since 1957. This agreement precedes the Treaty of Rome, and some Italians claim that it was originally introduced to mirror Japanese restraints on imports of Italian cars. The Japanese have since 1976 liberalized. In 1987, however, only 2,550 cars and 750 off-road vehicles were directly imported by Italy from Japan, although some Japanese cars are allowed into the Italian market through free circulation from other member states under Community rules which, in principle, prescribe the free circulation of goods from third countries.[34] In 1988, Japanese imports to Italy via other member states amounted to around 20,000 units, but this was still less than 1 per cent of its market. Nevertheless, for Fiat, the threat is obvious. It currently supplies 60 per cent of the Italian market, this accounting for no less than two-thirds of its total West European car sales.

The French government operates an informal restriction by making it clear to the Japanese that their car sales should not top 3 per cent of its market. It reportedly limits direct Japanese imports to five manufacturers, Toyota, Nissan, Honda, Mazda and Mitsubishi.

The industry-to-industry voluntary agreement of the United Kingdom, which restricts Japanese car sales in its market to about 11 per cent of the annual total, looks positively generous in comparison. Spain and Portugal, which joined the Community only on 1 January 1986, have used high tariffs to protect their car assembly operations from imports of all types, not just those from Japan. Tariffs are being reduced, but slowly.

This leaves West Germany as the only major West European market entirely open to the Japanese. In West Germany, both the government and the motor industry have traditionally preferred no protectionist measures to be imposed. It exports more than half its total output and stands to lose more than any other country, should a 'car trade war' break out. As the major open market in the Community, however, West Germany benefits the most from Japanese self-imposed export restraints.

In European countries unprotected by quotas – and admittedly without a domestic motor industry – the Japanese have shown how well their cars sell. In Ireland, Finland, Greece and Norway, Japanese cars account for around 40 per cent of new car sales, and in Austria, Denmark and Switzerland for more than 30 per cent (see Table 23).

Not surprisingly, there have been uncertainties about Community policy towards imports of vehicles from Japan after 1992. The Commission is having difficulty formulating proposals which can satisfy the widely differing views of governments and car manufacturers in member states. France and Italy have been aggressive in championing a tough line against Japan. Raymond Levy, chairman and chief executive of Renault, stressed that trade barriers were needed around Western Europe and existing French protectionist measures should be kept until 'lasting if not eternal' European measures had been introduced. He added, 'Europe must defend itself, but if Europe takes no measures, I want France to stand alone defending itself.[35] Vittorio Ghidella, Managing Director of Fiat, said that his company was happy to face competition from the Japanese when they started producing vehicles on the same basis as European manufacturers.[36] In the

Table 23 Japanese car makers' market share (units '000)

	1973	1975	1980	1983	1985	1986	1987	1988	
	%	%	%	%	%	%	%	%	Units
W. Europe	—	—	—	—	—	—	—	11.1	1,446
FRG	1.1	1.7	10.4	10.6	13.1	15.0	15.1	14.8	414
UK	5.6	9.0	11.9	10.7	10.8	11.1	10.9	11.3	251
Netherlands	11.4	15.5	26.4	23.4	22.3	24.4	25.7	27.5	133
Switzerland	10.0	8.4	22.7	27.2	25.2	26.7	28.7	31.1	100
Bel./Lux.	12.1	16.5	25.8	21.9	18.9	20.3	20.4	20.5	95
Sweden	4.5	6.5	14.1	14.6	16.1	20.9	21.8	25.9	88
Austria	7.0	5.4	20.7	30.1	26.5	27.9	31.3	33.1	83
Finland	20.8	20.8	35.4	40.2	38.5	40.4	41.7	42.1	73
France	0.7	1.6	2.9	2.7	3.0	2.9	2.9	3.0	66
Denmark	8.6	14.7	30.9	31.1	31.8	35.1	34.7	32.9	29
Norway	18.8	28.4	39.1	36.0	34.0	35.0	38.2	39.3	27
Ireland	2.6	8.9	30.7	25.9	33.8	43.5	46.3	43.0	26
Greece	n.a	n.a	49.2	39.9	27.6	28.6	35.1	39.0	22
Italy*	0.1	0.1	0.1	0.1	0.2	0.5	0.7	0.9	20
Portugal	26.8	11.8	7.5	8.1	9.8	9.8	8.5	4.7	10
Spain	n.a	n.a	n.a	n.a	n.a	n.a	0.6	0.9	10

Source: CLCA, National Associations, and DRI.
*Estimate.

middle sits the United Kingdom, with an industry-to-industry agreement, and host to Nissan and Toyota's assembly plants. At the other end stand the Benelux countries, with no bilateral import curb.

The real puzzle is West Germany. It imported 414,000 Japanese cars in 1988, by far the largest number of all member states, and is the least keen to see tough action against Japanese imports. West German manufacturers, Volkswagen, BMW and Mercedes-Benz in particular, seem not to want to jeopardize their recent sales success and major share in the Japanese market (see Table 24). However, Commission officials have reportedly accused West German politicians and officials of opposing Community import curbs in public but supporting them in private.[37]

The automobile industry in the Community, in spite of widely differing views internally, has insisted publicly that suitable measures be taken to ensure that the objective of authentic free trade is reached, and that these measures take account of the huge imbalance in trade with Japan, particularly as far as the motor vehicle sector is concerned.[38] According to Giorgio Rampa, President of the CLCA, the measures could provide for a transitional period and national QRs within a Community framework.[39] The CCMC wants to replace the patchwork of national restraints by a Community-wide ceiling on Japanese car imports. It calls for the ceiling to be lowered by taking as its base-line 1985-6, when Japanese cars and commercial exports to the Community totalled 1.05 million units, instead of 1987 when they totalled 1.1 million units.

In the light of these arguments within the industry, in October 1988 the Commission adopted a document giving political and strategic guidelines for the automobile sector prior to the completion of the internal market.[40] It has two objectives: first, to develop a policy on the long-term restructuring of the European industry; and, second, to address the issue of imports. Thus it seeks to persuade Japan to stabilize its car exports to the Community until the end of 1992 and moderate them for a limited period after that, in order to redress the persistent imbalance in the market. Commission officials have reportedly said that during this period bilateral restraints on Japanese car imports (both QRs and VERs) to France, Italy and the United Kingdom and Spain should be dismantled, and that these national restraints should be replaced by a Community-wide moderation accord, possibly in the form of a Community quota, for a further short transitional period.[41] Michihiko Kunihiro, an official of the Japanese government, has observed: 'It is being rumoured – and I most certainly hope that it is only a rumour – that some transitional measures are being considered to limit the imports of Japanese automobiles beyond 1992 on an overall basis, as the car market within the Community is being unified. Japan is seriously concerned over this issue and regards it as a test case of the Community's sincere commitment to truly opening its markets to the outside world'.[42]

In May 1989, the Commission reportedly decided to propose to member states and the Japanese government that the bilateral restraints on Japanese car imports should be eliminated by the end of 1992; for an 'additional interim period' beyond 1992, these restraints should not be replaced by a Community-wide quota, but 'Japan would continue to monitor the growth of its exports at Community level, in order to make progressively possible increased access to the Community market'.[43]

If the single market programme goes according to plan, frontier controls inside the Community have to be removed after 1992. Currently exports of Japanese cars and commercial vehicles to five member states are limited by varying types of restraints at the national level, and the curbs cover not only direct Japanese exports to each of the five states but also indirect exports routed through member states. However, such measures will be unworkable after 1992, because the removal of internal frontier controls will make them impossible to enforce.

For the Community, however, simply to allow the Japanese a free run of its single market is regarded as politically out of the question, at least in the foreseeable future, so the search is on for an alternative.

Table 24 Registered vehicles imported into Japan, 1983-8

	1983	1984	1985	1986	1987	1988	Growth rate 1987-88	Market share 1987	1988
United Kingdom	2210	2269	2513	4033	6771	9789	+44.6	6.9	7.3
Mini (Rover)	1611	1547	1626	2752	4507	6733	+49.4	4.6	5.0
Jaguar/Daimler	331	414	426	603	953	1652	+73.3	0.9	1.2
Rolls-Royce	51	71	74	127	242	280	+15.7	0.2	0.2
West Germany	26,787	32,634	40,157	53,916	74,289	91,648	+23.4	75.9	68.6
Volkswagen	9664	10,239	12,987	16,067	23,740	27,947	+17.7	24.3	20.9
BMW	6298	8854	11,766	15,250	21,015	26,826	+27.7	21.5	20.1
Mercedes-Benz	6428	7488	9194	13,820	18,749	22,625	+20.7	19.2	16.9
Audi	3563	5372	5391	7717	8772	11,342	+29.3	9.0	8.5
Porsche	535	518	619	831	1676	2434	+45.2	1.7	1.8
Opel	24	70	111	157	292	449	+53.8	0.3	0.3
France	703	871	1009	1729	3933	6153	+56.4	4.0	4.6
Citroen	427	495	635	924	1757	2417	+37.6	1.8	1.8
Peugeot/Talbot	19	26	62	402	1274	2364	+85.6	1.3	1.8
Renault	237	344	311	403	902	1371	+51.9	0.9	1.0
Italy	1696	2242	2492	3046	3832	4216	+10.0	3.9	3.2
Fiat	580	816	814	1233	1672	2006	+19.9	1.7	1.5
Lancia	60	138	104	128	339	645	+90.3	0.3	0.5
Autobianchi	739	932	1236	1311	1127	544	-51.7	1.6	0.4
Alfa Romeo	104	119	77	73	134	415	+209.7	0.1	0.3
Ferrari	40	65	65	136	286	390	+36.3	0.3	0.3

EC total	31,396	38,016	46,171	62,724	88,825	111,806	+25.9	90.9	83.7
Sweden	1244	1490	2033	3151	4699	6737	+43.4	4.8	5.0
Volvo	918	1046	1489	2228	3265	4634	+41.9	3.3	3.5
Saab	325	444	544	923	1434	2103	+46.7	1.5	1.6
United States	2646	2382	1816	2345	4006	14,511	+262.2	4.1	10.9
Other countries	—	94	152	137	220	529	+140.5	0.2	0.4
Total	35,286	41,982	50,172	68,357	97,750	133,583	+36.7		

Source: Japan Automobile Importers' Association.

The car market of the future

In April 1987 Data Resources International (DRI) made projections from the hypothesis that national quotas had been abolished and replaced by a Community-wide moderation accord. In this simulation the actual situation in 1987 was compared with the one where the Japanese take 9 per cent of each individual member country's market. The market shares of the Community producers are simply redistributed in proportion. Under these hypotheses, production losses would be incurred by Italy (−4.6%), France (−2.3%) and Spain (−2.3%), while gains would be made by West Germany (+5.1%) and the United Kingdom (+2.7%). Assessed in terms of manufacturers, the same assumptions (which suppose an overall reduction in Japanese penetration) give an impact ranging from a 4.7 per cent production loss for Fiat to a 5.3 per cent gain for General Motors of Europe. Producers in France and Italy would find this outcome very difficult to accept.

The Commission is still worried about the fundamental weakness of the automobile industry, the most 'European' of industries, its productivity and efficiency in particular, although these have improved remarkably. According to an internal Commission study, productivity improvements enabled the West European industry to make 13 million vehicles with 1.8 million employees in 1987, compared with 12 million vehicles and 2.2 million people in 1980; it earned profits of about ECU 7.6 billion in 1987 compared with heavy losses in the early 1980s.[44] However, the study stresses that the recovery is based on fragile foundations: the industry will face difficulties if demand in Western Eruope weakens. It points out in particular that if import curbs against Japan by five member states were removed, and not replaced by Community-wide restraints, Japanese car manufacturers' share of the Community market could rise from 10.6 per cent in 1986 to 18 per cent in 1995 (see Table 25), adding that, 'Arithmetically, this increase of 1 million units in Japanese imports would equate to the disappearance of one of Europe's six main producers'.[45]

The Commission constantly emphasizes that the European automobile industry must continue to play its current leading role in the Community by maintaining its international competitiveness. It stresses that: 'Faced with Japanese competition, the aims of the American industry and emergence of new producers, the European industry must continue to adapt its industrial and commercial base which is vulnerable because automobile construction is heterogeneous and components manufacture dispersed'.[46]

The Japanese have certainly been left in no doubt that there is a limit to the number of car imports West European markets will take without crying halt. They have had to look for ways to establish themselves whatever restrictive walls may go up. The Japanese have so far invested much less in Europe than they have in the United States, but this pattern is changing. Nissan Motor began assembling cars in 1986 at its plant in Sunderland in

Table 25 Abolition of national quotas without any Community measures

	Japanese car sales (000's)		Japanese car share (%)	
	1986	1995	1986	1995
West Germany	412	458	15.0	14.7
France	57	409	3.0	17.0
Italy	3	301	0.2	16.0
United Kingdom	206	336	11.0	18.0
Bel./Lux.	91	118	21.2	22.5
Netherlands	138	139	24.2	25.6
Community-10	999	1961	10.6	18.0

Source: The Commission, *A Competitive Assessment of the European Automotive Industry in view of 1992*, Brussels, 14 October 1988, p.22.

northern England and started to export them to continental Europe at the end of 1988. Under present known plans, Nissan Motor will have developed an annual productive capacity of 200,000 cars at Sunderland by 1992, half of them for export. Thus it will account for around 15 per cent of car production and will be the second most important car exporter by volume in the United Kingdom, close on the heels of Austin Rover. Nissan also has a 70.4 per cent stake in Nissan Motor Iberica, a commercial vehicle operation in Spain.

In addition, Honda Motor has entered a joint venture with the Rover Group in which Rover will produce 40,000 Honda Concertos a year at its Longbridge plant near Birmingham from the autumn of 1989. It is also building its own engine plant in southern England. Suzuki Motor has a 17.3 per cent stake in Land Rover Santana in Spain to produce its four-wheel drive vehicle Escood in 1990; the annual production target is 24,000 units. Toyota Motor has also an accord with Volkswagen AG under which Volkswagen began producing Toyota's one-tonne pickups under licence at its Hanover plant from January 1989; in 1989, Toyota and Honda unveiled plans to set up car assembly plants in the United Kingdom. These factories will produce 200,000 and 100,000 cars a year respectively.[47]

In view of this rapid increase in Japanese investment in the Community, the West European car manufacturers fear that further Japanese assembly plants would aggravate excess capacity in the Community markets, even though some manufacturers have mentioned experiencing difficulty meeting buoyant demand.[48] There is in fact over-capacity in parts of the Community industry, notably at Rover and Renault, but the more ambitious manufacturers, including Ford of Europe, are gearing up to create greater capacity.[49]

According to the world automotive forecast from DRI, the car markets of Western Europe, along with those of North America and Japan, appeared to have been at the peak of an unprecedented boom in 1988.[50] Sales in all the major West European markets were expected to decline in 1989, as a result of a widespread slowdown in economic growth and high interest rates depressing consumption. A senior official of the West European automobile industry admitted that 1988 had been a good year for its industry and that its manufacturers had been able to benefit from the strong demand in Western Europe, but he also agreed with DRI's forecast for 1989.[51] As Table 26 shows, car sales in Western Europe are forecast to decline by 5.8 per cent in 1989 to 12,037 million units, following an increase of 3.2 per cent in 1988 to a record 12,779 million units.

The Nissan case – local content requirement

The Community automobile industry is evidently wary of Japanese penetration of its market. Even Ford of Europe, one of the most aggressive and successful manufacturers in Western Europe, feels that a shake-out in the Community's automobile industry is unavoidable while the market is opened up to the full force of Japanese competition. It has pointed out that even Fiat, the most cost-effective of traditional West European manufacturers, will probably be overtaken by Japan's Nissan when the company's car assembly plant reaches the planned full production.[52]

Some anxieties within the Community industry first emerged in April 1982, when BL (now Rover Group) launched export production of its Triumph Acclaim, built in the United Kingdom under licence from Honda. Italy claimed that the British content of the Acclaim was only 60 per cent, not enough for the car to be called British, and held up imports. Since then, the industry has consistently asked the Commission for measures to ensure that Japanese assembly in the Community uses an adequate – but unspecified – level of local content and makes use of European research and development.[53] For example, Derek Barron, chairman of Ford in the United Kingdom, suggested in 1986 that to qualify as European, cars made in Japanese-owned factories in Europe should have at least 80 per cent Community content. He insisted that this should not be measured, as at present, by ex-factory value, which can include marketing costs and even profit, but by the actual cost of the product.[54]

It was against this background that in the autumn of 1988 Nissan Motor, the first Japanese manufacturer to establish its own car assembly plant in the Community, began exporting its Bluebird cars from the United Kingdom to continental Europe. However, as expected, France attempted to limit imports of these cars on the grounds that they should be classified as Japanese unless their European content was at least 80 per cent. This move followed huge protests from several automobile manufacturers,

Table 26 World car sales and production forecasts

Sales forecast (000's)

	1986	1987	1988	1989	1990	1993
West Germany	2829	2916	2730	2632	2699	2660
France	1912	2105	2217	1976	2035	2146
United Kingdom	1882	2014	2195	1963	1947	1939
Italy	1825	1977	2131	1957	1899	2002
Spain	686	925	1039	983	997	1089
Western Europe	11,635	12,380	12,779	12,037	12,207	12,622
United States	11,452	10,227	10,699	10,190	9822	10,623
Japan	3146	3275	3609	3359	3674	3497
World total	33,049	32,657	34,277	33,089	33,491	35,528

Production forecast (000's)

	1986	1987	1988	1989	1990	1993
West Germany	4311	4373	4339	4122	4173	4316
France	2773	3052	3178	2955	3049	3153
United Kingdom	1019	1143	1196	1185	1250	1362
Italy	1652	1713	1908	1811	1816	1813
Spain	1282	1403	1469	1379	1375	1422
Western Europe	11,818	12,518	12,917	12,245	12,444	12,939
United States	7730	7146	7163	6853	7158	7541
Japan	7810	7891	8040	7508	7752	7685
World total	32,727	33,098	34,312	33,440	34,400	36,174

Source: DRI.
Note: 1986 and 1987 figures are actual; 1988 to 1993, forecast. The world total excludes double counting.

Peugeot-Citroën in France and Fiat in Italy in particular, against the British government's decision to provide huge subsidies to help Nissan enter continental European markets.

The British government swiftly promised to back Nissan's export campaign and claimed that the French government was violating Community free trade regulations in barring British-built Nissan cars from the French market.[55] A spokesman for the Commission indicated support for the

British attitude and said that any attempt by the French government to impose restrictions on the import of British-built Japanese cars would be in violation of the Treaty of Rome.[56] The next day the French government lodged a bitter complaint with Jacques Delors, President of the Commission, over the Commission's intention to support the United Kingdom. In response, the Commission emphasized that it could not comment on the substance of this case, which was still under examination, and appeared to backtrack from what its spokesman had implied only a day earlier.[57] Thus French restraints on the sale of British-built Nissan cars rapidly developed into a revealing Community-wide row.

Interestingly, in October 1988, the French government conceded, in conformity with the Community's rules, that these cars could have free access to France once the model had been authorized.[58] The only question now was whether France counted the Bluebird imports as part of the quasi-annual quota for Japanese cars. This quota, as mentioned above, is not an official one, and France did not refer to it in its response to the Commission.[59] Later, however, a French distributor of Nissan cars produced evidence that its imports of these Bluebirds were being counted against its quasi-annual quota for direct imports from Japan rather than being admitted freely as European cars.[60] Meanwhile, in November 1988, the Italian government threatened to impose similar restrictions to the French against British-made Nissan cars;[61] the next month, Nissan told the British government that it was encountering the same restrictions on the Spanish market.[62]

But this lengthy dispute was nearly ended with a climbdown by France and Italy in April 1989. In reply to a request by Martin Bangemann, Vice-President of the Commission Responsible for the Internal Market, the French government indicated that 'the administrative measures required to ensure free access to the French market for Nissan UK Bluebird vehicles . . . have been taken', and confirmed that 'these imports from the United Kingdom will not affect the traditional imports of Nissan vehicles from Japan'.[63] However, the legal basis for France's insistence that British-built Japanese cars should contain at least 80 per cent local content to qualify as European products is not clear. A French government official explained the climbdown by saying that Nissan had reaffirmed an existing commitment to reach 80 per cent of Community content at its plant in the United Kingdom by 1990.[64] The Italian government has also undertaken to allow unrestricted entry to these Nissan cars, even though it continues to claim they are Japanese and not European because of 'the outstanding and unsettled issue of local content'.[65] In addition, in May 1989, the Commission indicated that 'should local content rules favour Community production over imported products, such rules would undoubtedly violate Article 3 of the GATT'.[66] It should be pointed out that these moves have important implications for the Community's car market, although the question is still far from final resolution.

Lord Young of Graffham, British Secretary of State for Trade and Industry, pointed out that the 'British-built Nissan car has reached 60 per cent European origin, qualifying it as a European car, and it should be accepted throughout the Community'. He emphasized that it was wrong for the French to count Nissan cars as part of its restrictive quota of Japanese cars.[67] The United Kingdom government had agreed with Nissan that cars produced in Sunderland would be treated as British products once their local content reached 60 per cent. In the middle of this Anglo-French row, Yoshikazu Kawana, a Nissan board member, said, 'These cars have been certificated by the British authorities as having been made in the United Kingdom. We were told that if we achieved 60 per cent local content then cars would be British made. Then it was supposed to be OK'.[68] Yutaka Kume, President of Nissan, said, 'The local content rate of our United Kingdom plant is already over 70 per cent and we are intent on raising it still further'.[69] By 1990, the Nissan Bluebird will have reached 80 per cent local content, enough to satisfy even the French unless new obstacles can be invented in the meantime.[70]

The French government has since explained the reason for its position. Roger Fauroux, French Minister for Industry, expressed it as follows:

The French and Western European automobile industry still needed three to four years to catch up with Japanese manufacturers. While the United Kingdom has always adopted a more flexible policy on Japanese cars made in Western Europe, France has felt the need to take a tougher line for as long as the car market in Japan remained virtually closed to Western European manufacturers. France could not afford the risk of large-scale lay-offs in one of its key industrial sectors by adopting a lax approach to Japanese car imports.[71]

French government officials also said that this dispute between France and the United Kingdom reflected the different economic weight of the automobile industry in the two countries.[72] Automobiles were no longer a strategic sector of British industry, but remained vital for France with its two large manufacturers, the private Peugeot-Citroën group and the state-owned Renault group. The French government appears to believe that Japan is trying to exploit the creation of the internal market in the Community and is using the United Kingdom as a Trojan horse by which to gain preferential access to the markets of other member states.[73]

The French and Italian automobile industries, the most strongly protectionist within the Community, naturally supported the French government. Raymond Levy, chairman and chief executive of Renault, said that the British-built Nissan Bluebird could only be considered a European car when it reached 80 per cent local content, and emphasized that, 'we say it is not a European car and we think it should not be circulating in Western Europe under a European label'.[74] Vittorio Ghidella, Managing Director of Fiat, in particular, argued that a detailed study of Nissan cars' local content revealed that only 20 per cent of their parts were clearly of European production; a further 30 per cent were ambiguous in that the origin and manufacture of the parts could not clearly be established as European, while the remainder was definitely of non-European origin.[75]

At any rate, in the absence of clear Community rules on local content, there was plenty of scope for the row between the United Kingdom and France over whether British-built Nissan cars should be treated as European or Japanese. The Commission is still divided over the percentage of the sales value which Japanese manufacturers should base on local content if their cars are to have guaranteed free access to the whole Community market. The Commission's position underlines the sensitivity of the case. Its outcome will have an impact on other Japanese plans to invest in the Community, which are already affected by the Council Regulation against the dumping of cheap components into Community factories.[76] Just after the French attempt to restrict Nissan car imports, leading Japanese automobile manufacturers were reportedly rethinking plans for investing in European assembly plants, although Toyota announced in early 1989 that it would set up its first European car assembly plant in the United Kingdom with the support of 'skilled and successful lobbying by the British government'.[77]

Even international rules on local content are generally reckoned to be ill-defined and incomplete, although trade officials realize that they are likely to play a growing role in future trade disputes because of the increase in cross-border investment flows and the rising importance of high-technology industries which draw on a multiplicity of sources for their final products. Yet the GATT has no specific regulations to define when and whether local content requirements can be used as an investment of trade policy. The subject is covered vaguely by Article 3 (5), which was inserted originally to regulate butter production, and outlaws the practice of establishing quantitative requirements on the production of goods. The international convention on how to define where a product originates is also extremely vague.

The basic yardstick the Community uses to define whether a product is locally made is that of the International Convention on the Simplification and Harmonization of Custom Procedures (the Kyoto Convention),[78] which it adopted in 1975.[79] It states simply that the substantial transformation which is economically justifiable should take place locally for a product to count as local, but it gives no specific percentage. Even now, Community rules state only that to qualify as a Community product, 'the last substantial manufacturing process or operation' and 'an important stage of manufacture' must be in the Community.[80] Thus many Japanese companies feel it politically advisable to strive for maximum local content.

However, the Community has overridden this in other sectors to introduce a specific 45 per cent by added value and parts on radio-receivers, television sets and tape recorders on the Commission Regulations in

December 1970 and April 1971.[81] On 22 June 1987, the Council adopted a regulation that 40 per cent of the parts used in assembly operations by companies of third countries found dumping in the Community should be of non-Japanese origin if assembled products were to escape dumping penalties as well as directly imported ones.[82] The Commission has demonstrated its willingness to see that this local content regulation is enforced, notably in response to Japanese companies' moves to avoid anti-dumping duties by establishing so-called 'screwdriver' plants in Western Europe.

The Commission's attitude is not necessarily justified, however, and may sometimes mask a desire to protect inefficient European manufacturers. The United States pointed out that 'protection of local industry is a powerful bread-and-butter issue in certain sectors (e.g. automobiles, electronic typewriters, ball-bearings)'.[83] In addition, protective measures of this kind may well undermine, rather than strengthen, the competitiveness and technological development of Community industries. As already mentioned, it may also tend to discourage necessary foreign investment. Michihiko Kunihiro pointed out that:

It has come to seem that the fortune – or the fate – of foreign investors who want to establish themselves in Western Europe will be increasingly decided by what has come to be called the 'European Content' Standard. This presents a serious problem. For many a company wishing to move plant from Japan it is imperative that it is able to manufacture products equal in quality to those produced in Japan. Because of this, it needs to be sure beyond question that it can obtain components of appropriate quality. Very often, however, these are not readily available from local suppliers. Factories need time to arrange for an assured supply of required components from local suppliers.[84]

The United States is also concerned about this issue. In a case involving local content in 1984, Canada forced US investors to adopt a local procurement policy in return for establishing themselves in Canada under the Foreign Investment Review Act (FIRA). Following a complaint by the United States against Canada, the GATT stipulated changes in FIRA on the grounds that the existing rulings led to discrimination against United States manufacturers who had to fulfil requirements not imposed on their Canadian counterparts.

The subject is scheduled to come up again in the Uruguay round of multilateral trade negotiations under the heading of Trade Investment Measures (TRIMs). The case of British-made Nissan cars may appear to be a parochial European squabble, but the question is typical of a whole range of international trade issues.

The 'screwdriver' regulation

On the issue of local content, it is useful to examine another controversial trade measure launched by the Community in reaction, undoubtedly, to Japan's successive trade and investment drives. This measure devises a new anti-dumping rule, the so-called 'screwdriver' regulation, designed to prevent non-member countries' manufacturers from avoiding anti-dumping duties by setting up 'screwdriver' assembly plants within the Community using dumped parts and components. Its aim is to offer West European manufacturers protection in the new cases where the Japanese industry based in Europe has acquired a competitive advantage.

The 'screwdriver' regulation was first introduced in July 1987 as an amendment to Council Regulation No. 2176/84, the Community's basic anti-dumping rule.[85] The new rule, Council Regulation No. 1761/87,[86] is said to be in part the outcome of more than a year's lobbying by industrial organizations throughout the Community,[87] which were becoming increasingly impatient with these 'screwdriver' assemblies. In July 1988, the Council replaced this new basic anti-dumping measure, Regulation No. 2176/84, with a single consolidated Regulation No. 2423/88.[88] This incorporates Regulation No. 1761/87 together with further amendments designed to clarify procedures and prevent non-member countries' exporters from weakening the effects of anti-dumping duties by bearing the cost themselves.

After a Commission press release on the proposed regulation was issued in February 1987, serious concern was expressed by the Community's trade partners, Japan in particular. Even member states were anxious about the impact that the restrictions might have on Japanese investments in the Community.[89] On 5 October 1988, Japan requested that GATT's anti-dumping committee conciliate the two sides. The next day it also called for the establishment of a dispute panel to adjudicate on this issue.

Regulation No. 2423/88 includes the following provisions. An anti-dumping duty is imposed on a product released into the Community market: (1) after assembly or production is carried out by a party which is related to or associated with any manufacturers whose exports of a like product are subject to a definitive anti-dumping duty; (2) where assembly or production was started or increased substantially after the opening of the anti-dumping investigation into the relevant product; and (3) where the value of parts or materials in the assembly or production operation and originating in the country of origin of the products subject to an anti-dumping duty exceed by at least 50 per cent the value of all other parts or materials used.

Although the rule contains no definition of the phrase 'related or associated', it is interpreted to mean that it applies to branch offices and subsidiaries, as well as to joint-venture operations within the Community between a member and non-member state's manufacturers, and to companies associated or cooperating with a manufacturer which exports a dumped product. An anti-dumping investigation may also be carried out into the activities of manufacturers other than those exporting the allegedly dumped product. However, the rule applies only if parts or materials from a non-member country represent more than 60 per cent of all parts and materials used in the dumped product.

The Community invoked its anti-dumping rule for the first time in July 1987 and imposed an anti-dumping duty against a Japanese product (ball-bearings).[90] In 1979, several Japanese products, acrylic fibres, saccharin, and stereo cassette tape heads, were in turn subjected to anti-dumping proceedings.[91] Thus, up to the early 1980s, Community industries' allegations of dumping by non-member countries' exporters mainly centred on raw materials, chemicals or relatively small and simple items such as fertilizers, fibres, ball-bearings and steel tubes.

However, since then the Commission has faced a growing volume of complaints by Community industries against Japan. These complaints are fuelled not only by concern about deficits in Community trade with Japan and high levels of unemployment in member states, but also by the threat to high-technology industries in the Community from the rapid increase of exports and investments by more successful Japanese competitors. In consequence, anti-dumping proceedings now affect more technically complicated items such as electronic typewriters, electronic scales, photocopiers, serial impact dot matrix (SIDM) computer printers, compact disc players and dynamic random access memories (DRAMs). Many complex questions have also been raised about the Community's anti-dumping methodology. It was in this context that the Community introduced the 'screwdriver' regulation, which, in turn, raised new, complex and difficult questions.

Since the 'screwdriver' regulation entered into force in June 1987, it has become highly questionable whether serious discrimination between Japanese and member states' manufacturers can be avoided. Otto Grolig and Peter Bogaert have put forward the following possible example:

There are independent and related manufacturers for specific products in the Community and there is a lack of alternative sources for key components (magnetrons for microwave ovens or lenses for photocopiers) for them. They have to import these components from a manufacturer in a non-member country in the same way and increase their production when the finished products imported from a manufacturer in a non-member country are subjected to anti-dumping duties. Then, an independent company, however, merely because it is not related to or associated with a manufacturer of finished products in a non-member country, can escape from the imposition of an anti-dumping duty.[92]

In March 1986, the Commission pointed out in its Communication to the Council that only a fifth of Japanese investments in the Community at that time were for manufacturing or assembly, and of this only a fraction involved a significant amount of value added locally; the remaining investments were directly linked to Japanese companies' export and trade thrust and the financial sector. Then it emphasized that: 'Further, more attention should be given to preventing investments limited to assembly operations in Europe of imported 'components' being effected for the purpose of circumventing existing anti-dumping measures'.[93]

In February 1987, Willy de Clercq, then Vice-President of the Commission, confirmed this in the press release annoucing the Commission proposal for the 'screwdriver' regulation: 'We have observed that whenever the Community opens an anti-dumping inquiry or imposes anti-dumping duties on a product, plants for assembling the product which is the subject of the inquiry or anti-dumping duty miraculously spring up in abundance in the Community'. He stressed that the proposal was not directed against Japan in particular, or any specific third country. In addition, Horst G. Krenzler, Director-General for External Relations of the Commission, pointed out:

[The Commission's anti-dumping regulation] is applied uniformly in all cases, irrespective of whether the exporter is in Asia, Northern America or elsewhere. . . . Since 1980 more than 390 anti-dumping investigations have been opened, of which 27 have concerned Japan. There have only been four proceedings (ball-bearings, electronic typewriters, photocopiers and printers) where significant duties have been imposed, and in three important cases (titanium, microwave ovens and cellular mobile radio telephones) no action was taken.[94]

The press release of February 1987, however, noted that the need to curb the operation of assembly plants within the Community after the imposition of anti-dumping duties on a finished product 'was found to be the case in particular for electronic typewriters, photocopiers, excavators and weighing machines originating in Japan'.

Brian Hindley pointed out that 'several indicators suggest that claims of dumping by the Commission . . . should be viewed as the latest attempt by the Community to solve what it perceives as "the Japan problem" '.[95] Recently, particularly since 1984 when Regulation No. 2176/84 was introduced, the Community has often been reluctant to accept price undertakings as alternatives to duty from Japanese companies found to be dumping, though previously such undertakings had been accepted. In July 1985, the Council refused to accept price undertakings for hydraulic excavators from Japan, saying that 'in this particular case . . . in the light of present trade relations with Japan, it is not in the interest of the Community to have recourse to price undertakings as an appropriate remedy for the injury resulting from dumped imports'.[96]

In May 1988, the Japanese government made a complaint to the GATT against the Community over its imposition of anti-dumping duties on

Japanese products assembled in plants within the Community. It pointed out that the duties discriminated between manufacturers associated with foreign enterprises and domestic manufacturers, even when the latter used the same proportion of imported parts in their finished products.[97] In September 1988, Muneoki Date, Japan's ambassador to the Community, pointed out that there was no local content requirement on European companies in the consumer electronics field, many of which were importing components from the same sources as Japanese firms operating in the Community.[98] On 21 November 1988, in fact, the Community imposed definitive anti-dumping duties on Japanese SIDM printers, but it took no notice of three of the four complainants which had imported dumped Japanese SIDM printers to resell under their own names.[99] It should also be noted that though three Japanese companies charged higher prices than those of comparable Community products, they were still made to pay anti-dumping duties because the Commission alleged that they were selling at a loss and therefore setting unfair prices.[100]

This discriminatory behaviour by the Community raises the question whether the 'screwdriver' regulation conforms with the GATT's Anti-dumping Code and the Agreement's regulations in general. In October 1988, the Japanese government requested that the GATT's anti-dumping committee try to conciliate the two sides, claiming that the Community's anti-dumping levies on Japanese products infringe the GATT's Anti-dumping Code. It also called for the establishment of a GATT dispute panel to adjudicate on the issue.

The Japanese government's fundamental position, presented to the GATT in May and October 1988, may be summarized as follows:

(1) The 'screwdriver' regulation requires companies of non-member countries assembling products in the Community to procure a fixed proportion of their parts and components (more than 40 per cent of the total product value) from the Community region. This is in effect a local content requirement and is consequently inconsistent with Article 3 of the GATT which imposes a standard of national treatment in respect of internal taxation and regulation. The Article proposes as the general principle for a standard of national treatment, that internal taxes and other internal charges, together with laws, regulations and requirements affecting the internal sale, offering for sale and purchase, and internal quantitative regulations requiring the mixture, processing or use of products in specified amounts or proportions, should be applied indiscriminately to imported and domestic products so as not to afford protection to domestic production.

(2) The Community has not assessed whether parts and components were being imported at prices below those charged by Japanese manufacturers on their home market, and has failed to substantiate 'injury' to

the Community's manufacturers. These factors are essential to the definition of dumping provided in Article 6 of the GATT. Instead, the Community has required of Japanese manufacturers assembling products in the Community that more than 40 per cent of their parts and components be of local manufacture. At the same time, insufficient account was taken of cases where the share of local value added was high and where the ratio of imported parts and components had been large only during the start-up period.

Even ordinary dumping cases provide several examples to corroborate these arguments. In its press release of May 1988, the Committee of Japanese Printers (CJPrint) claimed that the anti-dumping duties imposed against Japanese SIDM printers by the Community in May 1988 had been based on an unfair comparison. CJPrint stated:

The Commission appears to have found injury by disregarding the multi-criteria segmentation of the SIDM print market . . . and has examined only two criteria, print speed and number of pins, in calculating a price-undercutting margin for Japanese-produced printers. It is CJPrint's understanding that the Commission relied on an industry study prepared on its behalf by IMV-InfoMarkt, Düsseldorf, in finding injury and in establishing margins as the basis of its provisional duty determination.

The Commission's SIDM printer model comparison was based on the InfoMarkt study and the InfoMarkt's conclusions that certain heavy printers produced by the EUROPRINT [the Committee of European printer manufacturers] makers were 'inferior' to (less featured than) lighter printers produced by CJPrint makers.

Based on this conclusion and its own limited speed-and-pin criteria, the Commission assumed that the prices of heavier EC printers could be compared with lighter Japanese models. In doing so, the Commission's model comparison failed to distinguish for purposes of a price comparison heavy duty printers and light duty printers in the same speed range, despite the fact that heavy duty printers are as a rule much more expensive than light duty printers in the same speed range.[101]

In May 1988, when the Commission imposed provisional anti-dumping duties on imports of SIDM printers from Japan, it pointed out that the dumping margin, or gap, between 'high Japanese' and 'low Community' prices had varied from 4.8 per cent for Tokyo Electric, to 86 per cent for Fujitsu between April 1986 and March 1987, the period covered by the inquiry.[102]

In order to determine whether the provisions of the Community's anti-dumping regulation against 'screwdriver' assembly plants, Council Regulation No. 2423/88, are consistent with the GATT rules, Article 6 of the GATT and its Anti-dumping Code, a detailed appraisal is needed of both the wording of the GATT rules and EC practice in operating its own powers. Article 2 (6) of the GATT provides that 'in order to effect a fair comparison between the export price and the domestic price in the exporting country or the country of origin (which is referred to as the "normal value') . . . the two prices shall be compared at the same level of trade, normally at the ex-factory level . . . Due allowance shall be made in each case, on its merits, for the differences in conditions and terms of scale, for the differences in taxation, and for the other differences affecting price comparatively'.

The code also stipulates in Article 2 (5) that where there is no export price, this 'may be constructed on the basis of the price at which the imported products are first resold to an independent buyer'. It provides in Article 2 (6) that 'allowance for the cost, including duties and taxes, incurred between importation and resale, and for profits accruing, should also be made'.

The provisions of the code may be summarized as follows: (1) comparison between the two prices should be made at the ex-factory stage; (2) the export price is the sale to the first independent buyer, from which sales expenses and a profit in the exporting country must be deducted; and (3) other appropriate adjustments should be made in each case, on its merits, to ensure a fair comparison.

The Community's anti-dumping regulations against 'screwdriver' assembly plants follow these general lines, but add certain other adjustments to bring the prices to a fair comparable level. Important among these are 'selling expenses resulting from sales made at different levels of trade, in different quantities or under different conditions and terms of sale'. They go on to stipulate that deductions should be made for the following items: (1) transport, insurance, handling, loading and ancillary costs; (2) packing; (3) credit; (4) warranties, guarantees, technical assistance and other after-sales services; and (5) other selling expenses such as commissions and salaries paid to salesmen.[103]

For example, where export sales are made through an export subsidiary in the exporting country, the Commission deducts all expenses of the sales subsidiary plus a reasonable profit margin on the export price side, but does not deduct them on the domestic price side.[104] There is naturally a strong argument that such a procedure is inconsistent with the principle – which the Community itself emphasizes – of fair comparison.

Another problem is the deduction for overheads and general expenses. Article 2 (10) of Council Regulation No. 2176/84 provides that 'allowances generally will be made for differences in overheads and general expenses, including research and development costs, or advertising'. But this regulation has been repealed and the phrase is deleted in Council Regulation No. 2423/88. But in interpretation, the same basic line is maintained. The phrase means that the expenses in question are deducted on the export price side but not on the domestic price side; this makes the domestic price artificially high and creates another disequilibrium between the two prices; in other words, it produces a substantial increase in the dumping margin. This appears to be one of the main reasons why the Japanese government and industry argue that the Community's anti-dumping duties are based on an unfair comparison. (Brian Hindley has analysed the issues in detail in his articles in the *World Economy* of December 1988 and *The Financial Times* of 6 and 24 January 1988.)

The next problem is that the Commission calculates weighted average prices when establishing normal values. According to Clifford Chance, a consultant, these might be weighted average monthly or yearly prices.[105] The Commission, in effect, compares these weighted average prices with each individual export price. Whenever the export price is higher than the normal value, there is found to be a dumping margin of zero; whenever the export price is lower than the normal value, there is found to be dumping. A weighted average of all dumping margins is then calculated,[106] which is of course higher than the margin which would have been found if export prices above the normal value had been fully taken into account. Clifford Chance indicates that in this way *'it is possible for dumping to be found, even if the average export price is the same as or higher than the average normal value'* (emphasis added).[107]

It is also difficult to substantiate injury in cases involving circumvention of the Community's 'screwdriver' regulation, which provides in principle that the effects of the dumped imports must be assessed in relation to the Community production of a like product. Dumped imports involving circumvention must usually be shown to cause material injury to a Community manufacturer selling parts or components. Moreover, in the field of high technology, there are often not many suitable component manufacturers in the Community.

The Community manufacturing industry, and the high-technology sectors in particular, have undeniably suffered from the rapid expansion of Japanese products in the past few years. It is, however, doubtful whether the 'injuries' were caused by dumped products.

In February 1987, just before announcing its proposed 'screwdriver' regulation, the Commission stated that it had received a record number of anti-dumping complaints on a broad range of products including compact disc players, semiconductors, mobile telephones, etc., as well as electronic typewriters, photocopiers, excavators and weighing scales which were already subject to anti-dumping duties.[108] Whenever it imposes anti-dumping duties, the Commission argues that Japanese exports to the Community are growing rapidly and its market share is expanding to a marked extent entirely at the expense of its Community competitors. In August 1986, imposing provisional anti-dumping duties on imports of plain paper photocopiers from Japan, the Commission said that the Japanese market share had been growing since the mid-1970s and had reached 85 per cent in 1985.[109] In May 1988, when the Commission set out provisional duties on Japanese SIDM printers, it disclosed that imports of these products had risen from 800,000 units, 49 per cent of the Community market, in 1983 to 1.5 million units, or 73 per cent of the market, in 1986, while the Community exports to Japan had dwindled from 1,040 units to nothing over the same period.[110] According to one analyst, in May 1987 there were fifteen SIDM printer manufacturing plants in the Community, but in the following year the Japanese set up another ten.[111]

In the changing market situation, Japanese manufacturers have argued that Community manufacturers have a long history of conservative behaviour which is inappropriate for the rapid development of printer marketing strategies; in the end, they are the ones to suffer from their own high cost structures.[112]

The Japanese government and industry argue that when imposing anti-dumping duties on Japanese products the Community disregards the difficulty of procuring components locally. In March 1987, after the Commission had announced its proposal for Council Regulation No. 1761/87, Keidanren, the federation of economic organizations in Japan, sent letters to the heads of state and top officials of all member states and to the President of the Commission emphasizing that Japanese companies import components primarily to maintain the quality of their products, not in order to reduce costs and circumvent anti-dumping duties. It stated that:

Where local procurement of satisfactory parts and components was not possible at the beginning, they had to start their operation by assembling imported parts and components. Despite the effort made by Japanese firms to incorporate local parts and components in products which they produce in the EC, there are some major components which are not produced locally in the EC.[113]

The Community, meanwhile, responded to these arguments by saying that the legal basis for its regulation against 'screwdriver' assembly plants established by Japanese companies in member states was Article 20 of the GATT. The essential question was whether the assembly operation constituted a circumvention of anti-dumping duties previously imposed in accordance with the GATT rules.[114] Article 20 allows a government to take steps 'to secure compliance with laws or regulations which are not inconsistent with the provisions of this Agreement, including those relating to . . . the prevention of deceptive practice . . .'

The Community emphasized that Council Regulation No. 2423/88 (against 'screwdriver' assembly plants) was in accordance with existing international obligations, in particular those arising from Article 6 of the GATT, the GATT's Anti-dumping Code and the Agreement of Interpretation and Application of Articles 6, 16 and 23 (subsidies and countervailing duties) of the GATT. A number of senior officials in the Community have reiterated this position. In November 1988, for example, de Clercq wrote that, 'the Community has always supported the elaboration of internationally accepted rules in the anti-dumping area, as expressed in the GATT's Anti-dumping Code, and it has strictly applied these rules'.[115]

As for the adjustments or allowances in respect of differences affecting price comparability, the Commission has responded to the points raised, including those brought up by Brian Hindley. In January 1989, Horst G. Krenzler sent a letter to *The Financial Times* in reply to Hindley's article, spelling out the Commission's point of view.[116]

In his article, Hindley indicates that the Commission bases comparisons on the ex-factory level of trade, but, while it calculates the ex-factory price from the price of the first independent sale in Japan, it deducts only directly related selling expenses; on the export price side it deducts all the costs of the export sales company. He argues, therefore, that adjustment of the export price to the ex-factory level puts the (adjusted) export price at a different level of trade from the (unadjusted) Japanese domestic price, and that even if a Japanese manufacturer markets a product at identical prices in both Japan and the Community, 'the Commission will find a large dumping margin'.

Krenzler, however, maintains that this argument ignores simple economic sense and the GATT definition of dumping:

Economically speaking, dumping occurs where a producer, because of a certain isolation of his market, indulges in price discrimination between his domestic and foreign customers. Any such price discrimination cannot be measured by comparing price levels on two totally different markets. In fact, the conditions of the competition prevailing on these markets . . . can vary substantially, because of different structures, distribution and taxation systems. For this reason, Article 6 of the GATT states that dumping occurs where the domestic price . . . of a product is higher than the price for a like product, not when imported into the country of destination, but when exported from its country of origin. The point of comparison of prices is the exporter's factory gate rather than the premises of the buyer in either Japan or the Community.

He concludes that 'because substantial costs may be incurred between exportation and importation . . . the fact that prices are identical in Japan and the Community would be an indication that dumping was taking place'. Referring to the argument that the Commission's methodology provides 'the foundation for a major section of the Asia-facing ramparts of Fortress Europe',[117] Krenzler says that this ignores the fact that different situations require different treatment, and explains:

A marketing company in Japan assumes the functions of the producer's domestic sales department, whereas . . . the marketing company in the Community assumes the functions of an importer. . . . Whether goods are sold on the Japanese domestic market through the producer's sales department or through a related marketing company makes no difference to the prices charged. When the Japanese producer changes from selling to an independent importer to a related marketing subsidiary in the Community, the transaction is then based on transfer price, which is not reliable for a determination of a . . . sales price. Therefore the basis for determining the export price to the Community must be changed.

According to Hindley, however, the Community and Japanese marketing companies have exactly the same functions and the Community's methodology 'still produces a 30 per cent dumping margin . . . alternatively stated, the deficits in the EC methodology remain when the differences in function alleged by Mr Krenzler are accurately taken into account'.[118]

Another problem of Council Regulation No. 2423/88 is that it is capable of wider applications than the former Regulations No. 2176/84 and No. 1761/87, i.e. it applies not only to the new proceedings initiated after it came into force but also to the proceedings which were already underway but had not yet reached final decision.

In the light of this rather panicky change in the Community's anti-dumping rules, one fact is clear. Japan has moved so fast that industry and the administration in the Community have had difficulty keeping up. As a result, industry has been compelled to rely on high trade barriers and the Community has often been forced to devise formidable barriers to imports.

Rules of origin

Now, following the revised anti-dumping regulation against 'screwdriver' assembly plants, the Commission is hastening to draft 'rules of origin' on a range of sensitive products made by non-member countries' manufacturers. In February 1989, under new rules of origin launched by the Commission for integrated circuits, non-member countries' companies must conduct key manufacturing of the front-end process in the Community including diffusion operations 'during which integrated circuits are formed on a semi-conductor substrate by the selective introduction of an appropriate dopant'. Only if they comply with this regulation will products be guaranteed free circulation across the twelve member states as Community-origin products.[119] This means that if a manufacturer in a member state merely assembles and tests integrated circuits from imported wafers which have undergone diffusion in third countries, the products are not considered as made in the Community. The new rules in effect force US and Japanese manufacturers to build plants in the Community to make complete microcircuits for sale there. This requires enormous investment.

This rule was followed by a proposal from the Commission to the Council for a regulation defining the origin of photocopiers.[120] This would require that the assembly and manufacture of minor parts such as cables, drums, coils, side panels and screws are not sufficient to qualify the photocopiers as originating in the country where these operations are carried out. This draft proposal would supplement the basic regulation on origin, Council Regulation No. 802/68.[121] Article 5 of the Commission text defines the country of origin as that in which the last substantial or economically justified operation took place. Such a regulation would have a large impact on the Community photocopier market, which has a turnover of almost ECU 1 billion and is characterized by major imports, from Japan in particular which holds about 80 per cent of the market.[122]

A rule of this kind would in effect legitimize dumping duties on copiers assembled by Ricoh Electronics Inc (REI, the Japanese company Ricoh's US affiliate) and exported to the Community. In this case a complaint was made against Ricoh accusing it of dumping in 1985[123] and 20 per cent anti-dumping duty was subsequently imposed on its photocopiers bought direct from Japan.[124] The Commission now accuses Ricoh of getting round the duty by stepping up shipments to the Community of photocopiers assembled in the United States. Ricoh, however, issued a statement claiming that:

REI began to produce photocopiers in California in 1976. Currently, the company produces photocopiers and other articles. REI's principal market has been and remains North America. Only a relatively small portion of its production is exported to the Community. There has been no attempt to sidestep anti-dumping dutes. REI's production began ten years before these duties were imposed by the Community. Exports to the Community started as part of a world production and marketing strategy adopted by Ricoh in 1985.[125]

The Commission has proposed a draft rule on the origin of VCRs which would apply a 45 per cent added value criterion to the definition of origin. Similar rules are reportedly being prepared for other products such as computer printers and petroleum products.[126] It should be noted that Commission proposals have to be endorsed by a qualified majority of EC members in the Council of Ministers. The United Kingdom, for example, has resisted the proposal on photocopiers.

The Community's apparent intent behind such moves is to apply anti-dumping or import duties more strictly to companies from third countries. On these rules *The Financial Times* says: 'A new and poorly understood bogey is starting to add to Japanese and US companies' fears that the European Community might be tempted into greater protectionism as it builds its single market for 1992'.[127]

Muneoki Date expressed anxiety that, 'these developments lend credence to our suspicion that there is a strong undercurrent toward protectionism in the Community, despite many official declarations and assurances to the contrary. We cannot help being very apprehensive about 1992'.[128]

At the very least, these duties could raise the prices of the products concerned and adversely affect the interests of their consumers. In August 1988, deciding to impose provisional anti-dumping duties on VCRs imported from Japan and South Korea, the Community argued that 'a possible limited disadvantage to consumers with respect to the higher price of video cassette recorders (VCRs) . . . will be outweighed by the benefits of

Table 27   Community anti-dumping duties against Japan

Year & month	Product	Type of measure	Duty (%)
1983. 10.	Outboard motors	DD	22
1984. 7.	Miniature ball-bearings	DD	4 – 15
1985. 6.	Ball-bearings	DD	1 – 22
	Tapered roller bearings	DD	2 – 45
6.	Hydraulic excavators	DD	3 – 22
6.	Electronic typewriters	DD	21 – 35
8.	Glycine	DD	15
1986. 4.	Electronic scales	DD	1 – 27
1987. 2.	Housed bearing units	DD	2.24 – 13.39
2.	Plain paper photo-copiers	DD	7.2 – 20
5.	Outboard motors	DD-Conf.	22
1988. 4.	*Electronic scales & parts	DD-Ext.	†65.63
4.	*Electronic typewriters & parts	DD-Ext.	†21.82 – 56.14
5.	Electronic typewriters & parts (Kyushu Matsushita)	UT (DD – 1988.4)	
7.	Electronic typewriters & parts	UT	
8.	Video taperecorders (Funai & Orion)	PD	18
9.	Electronic scales & parts	C (DD – 1988.10.)	
10.	*Plain paper photo-copiers (Matsushita, Toshiba & Konica)	DD	†28 – 225
11.	Dot matrix computer printers (15 firms)	DD	4.8 – 47.0
12.	Photocopiers (Matsushita & Toshiba)	UT (DD – 1988.10.)	
1989. 1.	Serial impact fully formed character	DD	23.5
1.	Audio-cassettes & audio-cassette tapes	II	
2.	Photocopiers (Konica)	UT (DD – 1988.10.)	

Source: The European Communities, *Official Journals.*
Key: DD = definitive duties, PD = provisional duties, UT = undertakings,
C = cancellation, II = initiation of investigations, Conf = confirmation,
Ext = extention.
*Against "screwdriver" assembly plants.   † Ecus per unit.

safeguarding employment and maintaining a foothold in this important technological sector'.[129]

In no way can these anti-dumping measures be said to serve the interests of consumers of imported goods and their home-produced competitors. On the contrary, such measures almost invariably damage the interests of consumers. The Community since 1979 has maintained the 'interest of the Community' clause in its anti-dumping regulations.[130] The interest of the Community in practice tends to mean the protection of EC manufacturers challenged by imports but not the interests of consumers, import-using industries or even exporting industries. The Community position was delineated in the language used in 1985 in the Ricoh case (see Note 123). The motive was the lack of alternative policies by the Community or its member states to help local domestic manufacturers overcome the difficulties caused by highly competitive imports.

There is a real danger of preserving a high-cost Community industry, in electronics and other supposedly strategic sectors in particular, which is able to compete only inside member states, allowing consumers there to pay its bills but unable to compete against the Japanese in other markets. Such policies have done nothing to solve the Community's most serious and consistent industrial problem – its lack of competitiveness – and it therefore can be argued as being counter to the real interests of the Community. This is the crucial point.

5 Towards 1992

Japanese investment in the Community

The Community's anti-dumping regulation against 'screwdriver' assembly within the Community presents a serious problem to foreign investors. Not only non-member countries, Japan in particular, but even some member states fear that inappropriate application of these sorts of rules might discourage foreign investors.

In June 1987, just after the council endorsed its Regulation No. 1761/87, Hajime Tamura, the Japanese Minister of International Trade and Industry, expressed anxiety lest the new regulation slow down the flow of Japanese direct investment into the Community. He emphasized that many Japanese firms have a number of investment programmes in member states, but their plans could be seriously affected by the new rule.[1]

Japanese industrialists had a similar reaction. In March 1987, Keidanren stressed that the new regulation 'would greatly hinder direct investment from Japan in the EEC region', and indicated that, 'under such circumstances, Japanese firms would be interested in investing only in those countries where component industries appear relatively easy. This would mean that some of the EC member states which do not have a wide range of component industries would face a difficult situation, and foreign investment would be concentrated in a few countries and regions'.[2]

The United States also pointed out, in connection with the Community's local content requirements, that the new rule 'may mask a desire to protect inefficient European manufacturers', and would have a negative influence upon 'foreign investors who may lose some of their competitive advantages in the Community and in a potential export market'.[3]

Initial reactions to the new rule from the member governments were also cautious. Most accepted the need, at least in principle, to clamp down on the Japanese tendency to try to avoid anti-dumping duties by setting up low-cost assembly plants within the Community, but they were not necessarily comfortable with the measure. Ireland and the United Kingdom, in particular, were anxious about the impact such restrictions might have on

Japanese investment and the 75,000 jobs which Japanese leaders claimed they provided in the Community.[4]

In January 1987, when Samsung, the South Korean conglomerate, announced a plan to scrap its microwave oven plant in the United Kingdom, it cited the draft proposal for the 'screwdriver' regulation, Council Regulation No. 761/87, as a reason.[5] In 1988, Silver Seiko, the Japanese electronic typewriter manufacturer, abandoned production in the United Kingdom after the Commission imposed anti-dumping duties on its products under the 'screwdriver' regulation.[6] John Bedborough, the Managing Director of Silver Reed, the United Kingdom subsidiary of Silver Seiko, said the imposed duty of ECU 56.14 for each typewriter would add more than 40 per cent to unit costs in the United Kingdom.[7]

However, the Commission has consistently argued that 'the Community's main concern was to guard against the flagrant circumvention of anti-dumping duties while ensuring the provisions did not deter genuine inward investment'. It pointed out:

This aim seems to have been achieved. Direct investment from Japan into Europe increased by about 90 per cent in the year following the introduction of the provisions. Furthermore, in the investigation carried out, it was found that the assemblers have been able to switch the source of their components with comparative ease and once this happened the Community readily accepted undertakings from the assemblers and removed the duty on the assembled product.[8]

Since the early 1980s a new surge of investment has taken place within the Community. The main sources have been US companies, European-based multinationals or national companies of member states which have been stimulated by Western Europe's renewed economic strength to increase their competitiveness. However, Japanese companies, in particular, motivated to produce overseas by the consistently strong yen and the political need to close the country's trade gap, have been encouraged by the dramatically changed inward investment climate of the Community.

In 1977, Hitachi, Japan's electronics giant, planned to set up a colour television plant in Northern Ireland. But local industries and trade unions resolutely opposed the plan, perceiving it as a threat to local industries. Hitachi was consequently forced to abandon the scheme.[9] Nevertheless, there has been recognition of the potential importance of Japanese investment in the Community as a means of alleviating high unemployment in peripheral areas such as Spain, Scotland, Wales and the north of England. It could also be an accelerator of industrialization in rural economies, for example Ireland and Portugal, and a factor for correcting the Euro-Japanese trade imbalance in general.

Since the mid-1980s in particular, any sign that a Japanese company might be thinking of making an investment of this kind has been enough to trigger a stampede of national and regional development officials, armed with polished marketing pitches and offers of assistance.[10] Even France, which had never acknowledged Japan's industrial achievement and had maintained a hostile attitude towards multinational investments, particularly from Japan, ever since the Second World War, began to soften its attitude, stressing 'la solution japonaise'. With this new attitude from the French government towards attracting Japanese companies, the French manufacturing sector has the highest number of cases of Japanese direct investment in Western Europe (see Table 28). Attracting this inward investment is an increasingly high priority for the French government and industry as a means of revitalizing its domestic economy, strengthening the technological base of industry in particular, and increasing jobs and exports.[11]

The cumulative total of Japanese direct investment in the Community from FY 1951 to 1986 stands at $13,363 milion, 12.6 per cent of all investment, according to Japanese Ministry of Finance figures shown in Table 28. The United Kingdom received the greatest cumulative total of investment, $4,125 million, followed by the Netherlands with $2,337 million, Luxembourg with $2,308 million and West Germany with $1,552 million. The substantial sums invested in the Netherlands and Luxembourg were directed primarily into the financial sector to establish subsidiaries of Japanese financial institutions or to acquire local banks.

In the manufacturing sector, the United Kingdom was in the first place by value with $484 million. Investment in electrical machinery accounted for $178 million or 36.8 per cent, followed by transport machinery, such as cars, etc., with $97 million or 20 per cent (see Table 29). Spain was a close second with cumulative investment of $462 million. Approximately two-thirds, $301 million, went into transport machinery. France was in the third place with investments totalling $317 million. The main sectors were steel and non-ferrous metal, electrical machinery and textiles. West Germany came fourth with investments totalling $277 million, of which electrical machinery accounted for 46.2 per cent.[12]

Almost 30 per cent of Japanese investment in the Community in the past thirty-five years has been concentrated in the United Kingdom. In the first half of 1988, the UK was by far the most important recipient, accounting for nearly 60 per cent of Japanese money invested in the Community (see Table 30).[13] In early 1989, when Toyota decided to establish a car assembly plant in the United Kingdom, other member states, France and Italy in particular, criticized the British. For example, Renato Ruggiero, Italy's Minister of Foreign Trade, accused the United Kingdom of 'lacking solidarity' with its Community partners:

The courting of Toyota, following construction of the Nissan plant and Rover's collaboration with Honda, would undermine the Community's attempt to negotiate a car export restraint agreement with Tokyo, to come into effect after 1992. This is too much. The British are continuing to offer regional aid to highly com-

Table 28 Japanese direct investment in the Community (1)
(Cumulative total FY 1951-86, $m)

	Manufacturing		Non-manufacturing		Others	Total	
	No./cases	Amounts	No./cases	Amounts	Amounts	No./cases	Amounts
UK	287	484	725	3585	561	190	4125
FRG	149	277	620	1026	249	817	1552
France	309	317	379	536	117	742	970
Italy	51	100	87	70	33	156	203
Belgium	52	240	180	468	84	249	793
Netherlands	47	199	294	2134	4	354	2337
Luxembourg	1	4	98	2304	–	99	2308
Ireland	44	160	16	170	2	62	332
Denmark	5	2	32	15	0	39	17
Greece	8	94	8	1	–	16	96
Spain	87	462	58	63	76	163	601
Portugal	17	22	9	5	0	28	27
EC-12 total	1057	2361	2506	10,377	621	3915	13,363
USA	2610	9267	8886	25,080	1107	13,757	35,455
World total	11,847	28,206	24,580	74,285	3479	40,123	105,970

Source: Japanese Ministry of Finance.

petitive investors and setting them export targets to other European countries. It is like me offering money to Suntory to set up in the south of Italy and telling them to sell certain quantities in Scotland.[14]

There are very good reasons why Japanese companies have chosen the United Kingdom for their European plants. Of course English is the first foreign language for the Japanese. But more than language is at stake. When choosing a location for investment, Japanese companies consider 'the infrastructure, the liberalness of government policy and transparency of administrative regulations, the general investment climate and the friendliness of the social climate', as Muneoki Date put it, pointing out that, 'As concerns foreign direct investment, we are very much impressed and encouraged by the openness of both the UK administration and UK business circles'.[15]

According to him Japanese companies do not decide their investment locations 'on the basis of their gastronomic preferences for continental cuisine or other extraneous factors', adding that, 'You might have sensed a measure of jealousy on the part of other member states toward the UK, jealousy aroused by the fact that it has recently been chosen to receive new and important Japanese investments'. In a leading article, *The Independent* comments on Toyota's decision to build a car plant in the United Kingdom:

Nor will sentiment have played any part in the decision – unless the sentiment is taken to cover the misguided economic nationalism of France and Italy. These countries' deep hostility to Japanese investment has proved counter-productive. Yesterday [18 April 1989] it was learnt that France has abandoned its lengthy attempt to restrict the sale of Nissan cars built in the UK. Instead of gaining new factories which export a high proportion of their output to other European countries and obtain a high proportion of components locally, France and Italy will face additional competition from plants in the UK.[16]

During the first half of the 1980s, most Japanese manufacturing companies had a strong feeling that it was almost impossible to produce as efficiently in the Community as at home. The Community was both fragmented and idiosyncratic. Different countries' labour laws, their educational and training systems, and their technical standards, each rooted in its own industrial past, together constituted what was seen as an irrational constraint on management. According to the first survey carried out by JETRO in 1983, for example, many Japanese companies manufacturing in Western Europe were worried about the quality and punctuality of delivery of locally procured components with less strict managment and shortages of skilled local workers. They did not expect quick remedies to those problems.[17]

The notorious 'Poitiers affair' in 1982, when the French government ordered all Japanese VCRs to go through a tiny customs post at Poitiers (see p. 28), is cited as a milestone in changing Japan's attitude towards

Table 29 Japanese direct investment in the Community (2)
(Cumulative total FY 1951-86, $m)

		(a)	(b)	(c)	(d)	(e)	(f)	(g)	(h)	(i)	(j)	(k)
UK	(1)	25	8	120	45	44	11	34	6	363	185	171
	(2)	10	6	29	90	178	97	74	817	507	1389	872
FRG	(1)	—	14	2	58	37	3	35	—	556	9	55
	(2)	—	21	0	69	128	9	50	—	861	74	91
France	(1)	66	17	144	17	27	2	36	4	283	9	83
	(2)	48	18	56	48	52	6	89	55	343	26	112
Italy	(1)	14	5	4	9	3	2	14	—	75	1	11
	(2)	9	12	3	7	6	42	21	—	61	0	9
Belgium	(1)	2	9	5	6	4	3	23	—	127	14	39
	(2)	0	36	25	15	10	32	122	—	221	204	43
Luxembourg	(1)	—	—	—	—	1	—	—	—	7	74	17
	(2)	—	—	—	—	4	—	—	—	2	2181	121
Ireland	(1)	9	—	6	3	14	—	12	1	8	—	7
	(2)	104	—	6	1	28	—	21	17	5	—	148
Denmark	(1)	—	—	—	4	—	—	1	—	29	—	3
	(2)	—	—	—	2	—	—	0	—	14	—	1
Greece	(1)	—	5	1	—	—	1	1	—	8	—	—
	(2)	—	16	76	—	—	0	3	—	1	—	—
Spain	(1)	1	30	17	3	2	7	17	—	49	2	7
	(2)	19	44	24	7	58	301	9	—	60	2	1
Portugal	(1)	7	1	—	1	3	2	3	—	5	2	2
	(2)	8	1	—	1	1	6	5	—	2	3	0

		(a)	(b)	(c)	(d)	(e)	(f)	(g)	(h)	(i)	(j)	(k)
EC-12 total	(1)	127	95	308	157	149	34	187	11	1710	346	439
	(2)	200	222	257	262	495	494	432	889	2691	5295	1502
USA	(1)	112	247	172	455	518	123	983	119	5398	233	3136
	(2)	206	959	1156	1222	2618	1452	1584	762	8184	5974	10160
World total	(1)	1220	1356	1350	1500	1984	559	3878	965	10945	1215	11455
	(2)	2146	4337	5518	2597	4734	4201	4673	12424	14538	18099	29224

Source: Japanese Ministry of Finance.
Key: (a) Textiles; (b) Chemicals; (c) Iron and steel, ferrous metals; (d) Non-electrical machinery; (e) Electronics; (f) Transport machinery; (g) Other manufactures; (h) Mining; (i) Commerce; (j) Finance and insurance; (k) Other non-manufactures.
(1) No/cases.   (2) Amounts.

Table 30 Japanese direct investment in the Community (3)

	FY 1983 ($m)	1984 ($m)	1985 ($m)	1986 ($m)	1987 ($m)	First half 1988 ($m)	1951-87 ($m)	87/88 (%)
UK	153	318	375	984	2473	1985	6597	252.4
FRG	117	245	172	210	403	172	1955	192.4
France	93	117	67	152	330	149	1300	217.2
Italy	13	22	32	23	59	55	262	258.0
Belgium	126	71	84	50	70	55	863	139.5
Netherlands	113	452	613	651	829	662	3166	127.4
Luxembourg	265	315	300	1092	1764	353	4072	161.5
Ireland	3	1	81	72	58	15	390	81.3
Denmark	5	1	1	1	6	2	24	416.7
Greece	n.a.	9	35	0	0	0	96	—
Spain	52	140	91	86	283	50	883	327.9
Portugal	4	0	1	3	6	3	33	192.9
EC-12 total	944	1651	1851	3324	6201	3501	19,643	189.0
USA	2738	3359	5395	10,165	14,704	11,430	50,159	144.7
World total	8145	10,155	12,217	22,320	33,364	22,857	139,334	149.5

Source: Japanese Ministry of Finance.

investment in the Community. There also seems little doubt that the Community-wide restraints on VCR and television tube imports which followed the 'Poitiers affair' have promoted the spread of Japanese assembly plants in the Community. Since then, many Japanese have come to believe that the Commission might pursue a similar strategy in other product sectors. Since the mid-1980s, its imposition of stiff anti-dumping duties on Japanese electronic typewriters, excavators, electronic scales and photocopiers, and threatened moves over microwave ovens and computer printers, have all been viewed from Japan as part of a deliberate campaign to encourage increased investment in the Community's manufacturing.

At the same time, a number of member state governments have been prepared to shoulder an appreciable share of project costs through incentives such as regional development aid, training grants, tax breaks and research and development support. Until the mid-1980s, incentives were largely the prerogative of poorer countries such as Ireland, which still offers some of the most generous financing. But they have since been adopted in Europe's most prosperous industrial heartland, such as Austria, the Netherlands and several West German states.

The Commission has feared that intense competition between governments to subsidize inward investment might create the absurd situation in which the Community was attempting to compensate the Japanese with one hand for retribution which it administered with the other. It has, therefore, been trying to tighten up rules wherever it can. In March 1986, the Commission pointed out that:

In order to attract as much investment as possible in manufacturing, national and regional authorities in Europe have often been led into competition with each other, each offering bigger or more advantageous subsidies and other incentives. An exchange of views between the member states at Community level would thus seem necessary to counteract the tendency of Japanese investors to exploit these attempts at outbidding.[18]

In September 1986, de Clercq warned member states against using competitive state subsidies to attract Japanese investment, saying, 'We must improve coordination between member states so that we can limit this beggar-my-neighbour policy to attract new investments'.[19]

In its leading article of 19 January 1987, *The Financial Times* argued that 'Japanese investment in Europe has turned out to be more of a gift horse than a Trojan one. Yet largely because governments have used the stick of real or threatened import restrictions and the carrot of starting-up subsidies to bring in the beast, the "quality" of Japanese investment so far has been disappointing'. It concludes that such a 'contradictory combination of incentives' is a poor way of guaranteeing that the Community gets its fair share of commercially sound Japanese investment; and bidding contests between member states – and within states – is wasteful.

In a further argument for Japanese investment, the Commission indicated that 'only a fifth of Japanese investments in the Community are for manufacturing or assembly, and of this only a fraction involves a significant amount of value added locally. The remaining investments are directly linked to Japanese companies' export and trade thrust and the financial sector'. It stressed that:

Japanese investments should be steered towards manufacturing activities with a high value added so that Japanese interests become inextricably linked with a market of 320 million consumers, which already buys more than 20 billion dollars' worth of their finished products annually . . . . Furthermore, attention should be given to preventing investments limited to assembly operations of imported 'components' being effected for the the purpose of circumventing existing anti-dumping measures.[20]

Governments and industries in the Community naturally insisted that Japanese companies bring in their advanced technology and teach it to local workers, rather than relying on components or parts sent from Japan. Clearly following an example set by the United States, they have told Japanese manufacturers opening plants in the Community that they have to buy at least 45 per cent of their products' components or parts from local suppliers. Although this is far from constituting a general rule of local content throughout the Community, the Commission has often used a criterion of 45 per cent added value. In some cases the percentages demanded were higher. One example is the Triumph Acclaim, manufactured by BL (now Rover) under licence from Honda (see above). When exports began in April 1982, the Italian motor industry claimed that the cars' British content was only 60 per cent, not enough to entitle them to be called 'British', and the Italian authorities held up imports.[21] By 1985, with Nissan planning an assembly plant in the United Kingdom, industrialists began insisting on 80 per cent local content.

Such were the pressures behind the 'screwdriver regulation' introduced by the Community in June 1987 as an amendment to its basic anti-dumping regulations. In July 1988, it then launched Regulation No. 2423/88, consolidating the basic regulation with an amendment to strengthen its effect, as already noted. It is now drawing up 'rules of origin' on products made by non-member countries' manufacturers.

Nervous about these measures and about their role in the post-1992 unified Community, Japanese companies have been hastily trying to change their image and upgrade their operations in the Community by rationalizing production, stepping up research and development activities and moving decision-making powers to their West European headquarters. In the JETRO survey shown in Table 31, the reasons for entering the European market most frequently mentioned by respondents were to avoid trade friction and increase local content to prepare for the 1992 market integration, and to increase production bases in Europe.

Table 31 JETRO's survey 1988 (1)

What are your motivations and reasons for starting to produce in Europe?

	(a)	(b)	(c)	(d)	(e)	(f)	(g)	(h)	(i)	(j)	(k)	(l)
Food	10	4	5	—	3	1	4	—	—	—	4	2
Textiles	4	4	1	—	—	—	3	—	1	—	1	1
Pulp & paper	1	1	—	—	—	—	—	—	—	1	—	1
Chemicals	29	20	8	2	4	6	4	2	1	9	7	1
Pharmaceuticals	5	4	1	1	—	—	1	1	—	—	1	1
Rubber products	8	1	—	1	—	3	2	—	4	1	2	3
Ceramics	4	4	1	—	—	1	1	—	—	1	—	—
Non-ferrous metals	2	2	—	—	—	—	—	1	—	—	—	—
Metal products	9	5	1	1	—	3	1	—	—	1	5	2
General machinery	25	9	3	13	1	5	2	2	5	3	7	6
Electronics*	71	29	8	37	—	9	12	11	19	14	19	9
Transport†	17	7	—	6	—	3	—	5	2	—	—	6
Precision‡	5	3	1	2	—	2	1	1	—	—	3	—
Other	26	20	2	4	2	2	8	2	—	4	15	1
Total	216	113	31	67	10	35	39	25	32	34	64	33

Source: JETRO, *The Current Management Situation of Japanese Manufacturing Enterprises in Europe*, Tokyo, March 1989, p.36.

Key: (a) Total; (b) Developing new markets; (c) Reducing production costs; (d) Avoiding trade friction; (e) Acquiring cheap raw materials; (f) Avoiding the risk of exchange rate-fluctuations; (g) Building up overseas market information capabilities; (h) Preparing for the 1992 market integration; (i) Maintaining orders from sales subsidiaries or the parent company; (j) Preferential tax treatment; (k) Meeting the diversified needs of consumers; (l) Other.

*Electronics and electrical equipment.

†Transport machinery. ‡Precision machinery.

In fiscal year 1987 (to the end of March 1988), Japanese direct investment in the Community rose by 89 per cent from the previous year (see Table 30). However, total direct investment overseas also rose sharply – investment in Asia soared by 109.2 per cent from the previous year. The rapid growth of Japanese investment overseas could therefore be part of a general tendency based on factors such as the appreciation of yen, the globalization of the Japanese economy and certain frictions with its trading partners. Nevertheless, the leap in investment in the Community was undeniably motivated to some extent by Japanese companies' plans to establish a foothold in advance of 1992, because they fear exclusion after that date. But as de Clercq has pointed out, there is at present no clear evidence that the 'screwdriver' regulation is a major factor in the fast growth of investment in the Community.[22]

The Community's local content standard and 'screwdriver' regulation have posed new problems for Japanese companies wishing to move plant from Japan to the Community. They have to be able to manufacture products equal in quality to those produced in Japan, and so they need to be absolutely certain that they can obtain components of the appropriate quality. But even now these are not readily available from local suppliers in the Community. Thus, Japanese companies still have problems with the quality, price and delivery of local components. Don Pinchbeck, General Manager of Epson UK, says the Community's local content requirement and new anti-dumping rules have forced companies like his to develop local content too fast for efficiency.[23]

According to the JETRO survey, the majority of Japanese respondents, coming from highly sophisticated assembly industries – electronics and electrical equipment companies particularly – are still dissatisfied with the local sub-contractor companies on grounds of quality, delivery and so on (see Tables 32 and 33). The local content ratio in these highly sophisticated assembly industries is much lower than in industries such as chemicals.

Pinchbeck records that Epson has experienced serious difficulties in finding plastics mouldings for its computer printers:

We found that first of all local suppliers tend not to have the technology. . . . Epson has transferred technology into the supplier to enable the supplier to give us the quality that we need. But sometimes you cannot get the quality and there is absolutely nothing you can do about it.

The steel that we can find in Europe, the best quality steel that we could find, had a tolerance that was not as good as the steel from Japan. Because of that, when we fitted the other bits, the tie bars and so on, we found that they were slack. If we had left it that product would have lasted a year instead of six, seven, nine or ten years. We cannot get steel of the quality that we need in Europe.[24]

According to Pinchbeck, Epson has, however, had to buy steel in Europe; consequently its costs have been increased by 'millions of pounds', forcing it to run down its research unit in the United Kingdom.

Table 32 JETRO's survey 1988 (2)
Are you satisfied with the present sub-contractor companies in terms of quality, delivery term and so on?

	Yes	No	No response
Food	2	0	0
Textiles	1	0	0
Chemicals	2	1	0
Pharmaceuticals	0	1	0
Rubber products	0	3	0
Non-ferrous metals	0	1	0
Metal products	0	1	0
General machinery	6	10	0
Electronics & electrical equipment	10	32	1
Transport machinery	1	11	1
Precision machinery	1	3	0
Other	6	4	0
Total	29	67	2

Source: JETRO, *The Current Management Situation of Japanese Manufacturing Enterprises in Europe,* Tokyo, March 1989, p.48.

Table 33 JETRO's survey 1988 (3)
If you are not satisfied, please describe why not.

	Quality	Price	Delivery	Other	No response	Total not satisfied
Chemicals	1	—	—	—	—	1
Pharmaceuticals	1	1	1	—	—	1
Rubber products	2	3	1	—	—	3
Non-ferrous metals	1	—	—	—	—	1
Metal products	1	1	—	—	—	1
General machinery	7	6	6	—	—	10
Electronics*	25	23	21	—	—	32
Transport †	7	7	8	1	1	11
Precision ‡	3	—	2	—	—	2
Other	3	—	3	—	—	4
Total	51	41	42	1	1	66

Source: JETRO, *The Current Situation of Japanese Manufacturing Enterprises in Europe,* Tokyo, March 1989, pp.48, 49.
*Electronics and electrical equipment.   † Transport machinery.   ‡ Precision machinery.

The example shows how the Community's local content standard and 'screwdriver' regulation can block Japanese research and development efforts although these will be needed if the Japanese companies are to integrate with the Community economy.

Nevertheless, in the JETRO survey, 100 firms (46.2 per cent of 216 respondents) said that their local sourcing ratio of components and materials had increased in the past year, while 83 firms (38.4 per cent of respondents) said it had not increased. However, where there was an increase, it stemmed mainly from the firms' own efforts to find local suppliers.

Pinchbeck stresses that 'screwdriving is an interim thing in the development of a global industry'.[25] Muneoki Date also points out that the present Community approach takes into account only the short-term interests of certain industrial sectors and could prejudice long-term cooperation.[26]

Meanwhile, pressure from the Community's industries for greater protection keeps on growing. In November 1988, the French electronics industry association called for precise restrictive measures to protect its members from foreign investment, indicating that it wanted to see the Community's 45 per cent local content requirement for Japanese manufacturing plants increased to 60 per cent.[27] The French government is reported to have demanded that the Commission rewrite the Community rules on local content requirement, and declared unilaterally that Nissan cars assembled in the United Kingdom would be treated as Japanese imports – therefore subject to the French quota – until they had 80 per cent content.[28] Jacques Calvet of Renault even said: 'fixing the local content of Japanese cars made in Europe at 80 per cent is not enough. The level should be much closer to 100 per cent'.[29]

These attitudes are founded on the lack of competitiveness of the Community's industries, consumer electronics, information technology and some car manufacturers in particular. According to one report, leading electronics companies in the Community such as Philips, Thomson and Olivetti are urgently restructuring in an effort to stay competitive. Their future depends on their success in the internal market of the Community.[30] The report emphasizes that if their survival is threatened – in other words, if Japanese companies over-react to 1992 by competing too fiercely – 'the Community will move to a protectionist policy'. It says that there are strong protectionist forces 'in industry, in the European Parliament, at lower levels of the Commission and some national governments', though it does not believe that Community leaders want to build a 'fortress Europe'.

Reciprocity

Fears are growing among non-member countries, from industries to governments, that the integration of markets in the Community in 1992 will make it harder for companies of non-member countries to share in the wealth promised by the programme. This brings us to another critical issue, namely 'reciprocity': i.e., the question of whether in certain areas of trade the Community will seek to apply tests of reciprocal market access to its trading partners. The issue has been raised particularly in the services sectors not yet covered by the GATT. The Community has not yet adopted an overall approach, although reciprocity appears in several draft directives (not yet adopted) and public statements, some official, which give some indications of Community thinking. In July 1988, de Clercq, for example, took the following view:

The completion of the single market will create a tougher competitive environment. There is no *a priori* reason to suppose that the subsidiaries of American or indeed Japanese companies operating in the Community will do better or worse than European-owned companies. That will depend on the calibre of the management and the ability and flexibility of the work-force.. Those in Europe who express fears on this point are doubting the ability of our own management. Correspondingly, European companies, by reason of their lower costs and wide market base, will be in a stronger competitive position in their home market vis-à-vis imports from third countries and will themselves be in a stronger competitive position in international markets.[31]

This suggests that there is no need to fear that the integration of the Community's markets could result in discrimination against non-member countries, that is in restrictions on third countries' services, investment and public procurement. He added, however:

But it is important to remember that the GATT does not cover all international trade. When international obligations do not exist, we see no reason why the benefits of our internal liberalization should be extended unilaterally to other countries. We shall be ready and willing to negotiate reciprocal concessions with third countries . . . . We want to open our borders, but on the basis of a mutual balance of advantages in the spirit of the GATT.

In October 1988, the Commission emphasized that reciprocity 'is an internationally accepted principle of trade policy both in the GATT and in the OECD', and indicated that:

The Commission reserves the right to make access to the benefits of 1992 for non-member countries' firms conditional upon a guarantee of similar opportunities – or at least non-discriminatory opportunities – in those firms' own countries. This means that the Community will offer free access to 1992 benefits for firms from countries whose market is already open or which are prepared to open up their markets on their own volition or through bilateral or multilateral agreements.[32]

The starting-point of the discussion is what should determine 'national treatment' of firms operating inside the Community. Article 58, paragraph

1, of the Treaty of Rome stipulates that 'Companies or firms formed in accordance with the law of a Member State and having their registered office, central administration or principal place of business within the Community shall, for the purpose of this chapter [Chapter 2] be treated in the same way as natural persons who are nationals of Member States'. Chapter 2 provides the 'Right of Establishment' (Articles 52-8). According to experts, this right is 'economically and legally speaking the right for a person or body, corporate or uncorporate, bearing the nationality of one State to cross into another State, and establish himself or itself there either by agency, branch, subsidiary, etc.[33] Such freedom of establishment is generally understood to relate to all Community nationals, whether national or legal persons.[34] This understanding also applies to 'freedom to provide services' (Chapter 3 of the Treaty of Rome).

Under Community rules, therefore, no member state is allowed to restrict the freedom of these companies or firms to set up new subsidiaries or branches elsewhere in the Community. In other words, all that even companies or firms of non-member countries have to do is to choose a place where they are accepted. However, the 1992 programme seeks to extend the freedom to provide services across the Community and to ensure that this freedom can be exercised by all Community firms. The issue, however, is whether this freedom should also apply to firms owned by third countries.

The idea of reciprocity-based trade policies first became popular in the United States, the principal architect and supporter of the GATT system, in the mid-1970s. In the 97th Congress (1981-2), for example, more than thirty bills were introduced calling for United States government action to achieve 'reciprocity in foreign trade'. According to William R. Cline, the United States reciprocity objectives originally meant 'seeking reciprocal changes in protection in negotiations', but this changed to seeking 'reciprocity in the level of protection bilaterally and over a certain range of goods'.[35] In 1982, Senator Robert Dole wrote that reciprocity 'means that other countries should provide us with trade and investment opportunities equal not simply to what they offer their other most favoured trading partners, but equal to what we afford them'.[36]

Most favoured nation (MFN) treatment means the principle of non-discrimination, the basic rule of GATT for trade in goods. Reciprocity seems, therefore, to have been urged as an alternative to MFN treatment.[37] The premise underlying this move to reciprocity in the US Congress was that, after decades of US leadership in trade liberalization, 'the result is an American market with comparatively few import barriers while foreign markets are protected by a variety of restrictions'.[38] The ensuing reciprocity legislation aimed at restoring the United States' bargaining position by the threat of retaliation. Needless to say, this trend is inconsistent with the principal rules of the GATT as set out in Article 1, because treatment would no longer be uniform across suppliers.[39]

Nevertheless, the move towards reciprocity gained ground with the Reagan Administration's new trade policy in September 1985. This meant frequent invocation of Section 301 of the Trade Act of 1974 providing authority to reduce unfair trade practice abroad, and the so-called 'Super 301' of the Trade Act of 1988, which mandates the United States Administration to retaliate against countries whose trade practices are judged unfair. The idea of reciprocity is becoming increasingly popular elsewhere, including the Community.

The Community's definitions of 'reciprocity' have risen particularly in the context of service liberalization and are not yet fully refined. The Commission defines it only as 'a guarantee of similar opportunities – or at least non-discriminatory opportunities' for member states' companies to operate in non-member countries' markets on the same basis as local companies. It has emphasized that 'it does not mean that all partners must make the same concessions nor even that the Community will insist on concessions from all its partners'.[40]

This explanation, however, appeared to be merely a temporary answer for foreign anxieties that the Community might seek 'mirror-image' rules of access from non-member countries before letting their companies into its own market. Fears had been aroused by somewhat provocative statements made by de Clercq, for example, 'the Commission will check on a case-by-case basis whether similar institutions from all member states are given the same treatment in the non-member country concerned . . . in many cases, we will have to pursue a symmetry not so much in the legal equivalence of conditions of access to markets, but rather an equivalence in their economic effects'.[41]

These remarks have naturally caused considerable controversy. In August 1988, Peter McPherson, then United States Deputy Secretary of the Treasury, pointed out that there are always differences between different countries' institutions, between financial sectors and in the scope of permitted operations, regulations, market instruments, methods of financing public debt, etc. He emphasized that the application of a 'mirror-image' standard would mean that 'legitimate differences in national regulatory regimes could be used to justify discrimination against foreign firms'. This would set the Community on a collision course with the United States.[42]

This argument, and the United States Administration's position on this matter, is explained in its public discussion document as follows:

[The Commission's suggestion] could result in restrictions on firms of countries that are unwilling to grant EC firms better than national treatment or to adopt laws or regulations equivalent to those that will govern activity in the single EC market. In areas where nations have differing views on how best to serve and protect the public, national and regulatory systems will reflect those differences. Because countries are unlikely to adapt their systems to suit the demands of foreign governments, mirror-image reciprocity results in discrimination, even against countries with open, non-discriminatory regulatory systems. Foreign firms operating in the EC would be placed at a competitive disadvantage with respect to EC firms.[43]

The Japanese government takes almost the same position on the matter. In October 1988, Michihiko Kunihiro said: 'In today's world, different legal and social systems exist for many justifiable reasons. As a result there are often instances when benefits cannot be exhanged quid pro quo. To withdraw a benefit each time the other country cannot reciprocate, would diminish the scope of free trade very seriously and lead to the opposite of what we should be achieving'. He asked the following question:

For example, when Nippon Telegraph and Telephone Corporation (NTT) was privatized and liberalized, Japan's telecommunication services market was made open equally to all countries. What would have been the situation if Japan had decided not to open its market to West Germany and France where the telecommunication services are still monopolized by the governments, while opening the Japanese market to Britain where it is open?[44]

Following these criticisms, the Commission appears to have been forced to retrench from de Clercq's position. In October 1988, Kenzler dismissed as misleading the idea that the Community sought rigid 'mirror-image' reciprocity. He stressed that the Community would apply a broadly defined reciprocity requirement when deciding whether to permit firms from non-member countries to have access to its unified market after 1992.[45]

The Community first introduced a reciprocity-based policy to the financial services sector with the Commission's proposal for a Second Banking Coordination Directive.[46] It should be recognized that this proposed Directive, like the proposed Investment Services Directive, contains many positive features.[47] For example, they would create a single licence, valid for both the establishment and provision of financial services throughout the integrated European market by the end of 1992. Licensing and prudential supervision of financial institutions would generally be the responsibility of each member state. The Council Directive on the Liberalization of Capital Movements, which the Council adopted on 24 June 1988, also provides for the removal of essentially all intra-Community restrictions on capital movements.[48]

Since it was sent to the Council in January 1988, the proposed Second Banking Coordination Directive has been causing controversy both within the Community and on account of Article 7 which stipulates that non-member countries' institutions should be subjected to a reciprocity test before they can be admitted. The same provision is contained in Article 6 of the proposed Investment Services Directive. These provisions may be summarized as follows.

A financial institution in a non-member country wishing to set up a subsidiary in the Community would file the relevant application for a licence with the competent authority of the member country; but the actual granting of the licence by that authority would depend on a Community procedure to evaluate whether all financial institutions of the Community enjoy reciprocal treatment in the applicant's country, and what corrective measures might be taken if this is not the case.

These proposed directives appear to be inward rather than outward-looking and consequently, as Anthony Loehnis, head of the international division of the Bank of England, points out, they conflict with what should be the primary objective of providing the Community with a competitive and innovative framework within which domestic and international financial services are available to customers.[49] It should also be noted that ':the non-discretionary, automatic and bureaucratic procedure proposed by the Commission for holding up authorization of financial institutions for any non-EC country until it has established that institutions from all member countries have reciprocal access to the third country hardly seems consistent with a commitment to liberalization within the Community and without'.

The Council of Ministers for Economic and Financial Affairs on 7 November 1988 was deeply split into two camps over the proposed Second Banking Directive; several northern countries including the United Kingdom, West Germany, Luxembourg and the Netherlands were, as West German Finance Secretary Hans Tietmayer said, 'very sceptical about the principles and practice of reciprocity' in international banking, while only France showed itself to be very attached to international reciprocity'.[50]

De Clercq then gave a new impetus to the controversy already stirred up by the proposed Directive. He suggested that financial institutions of non-member countries would not automatically be free to benefit fully from the planned single market in financial services, even if they were already licensed to operate in a member state.[51] In other words, reciprocity might be applied retroactively. While de Clercq seems to have been voicing the French, rather than the 'northern' view, the Italians go even further, asserting that reciprocity entails identical or 'mirror-image' treatment. This amounts to a call for global harmonization.[52]

It is questionable, however, whether there is a legal basis for discriminating in this way against companies or firms formed in accordance with laws of a member state whose parent companies are outside the Community. The interpretation of those Articles in the Treaty of Rome which refer to rights of establishment – particularly Article 58, paragraph 1 – is at present under discussion within the Community.

The Commission's proposal for a Second Banking Directive stated clearly that 'third country banks which establish their *subsidiaries* in any Community country are considered as Community undertakings as of the moment of their incorporation (Article 58 of the Treaty) and therefore may benefit from rights of establishment and free provision of services within the territory'.[53]

In September 1988, Geoffrey Fitchew, Director-General of the Commission's Economic and Financial Affairs Division (DG II), said that the Commission's proposal could not be used to restrict operations of institutions from outside the Community already established in a member state. He stressed that it was absolutely clear that it would apply only to new licences issued to non-member countries' institutions after 1992.[54]

In October 1988, the Commission itself confirmed officially that: 'The Second Banking Directive being discussed by the Council provides for the possibility of reciprocity for newcomers. However, there can be no question of depriving the subsidiaries of foreign firms already established in Community Member States of the rights they have acquired.[55] The definition of 'newcomer', however, is not clear.

Against this background, in April 1989, the Commission adopted a revised proposal for a Second Banking Coordination Directive to simplify the procedure for individual banking applications and clarify the 'reciprocity' provisions governing the establishment in the Community of subsidiaries of third-country banks.[56] The Commission wishes to revise the main elements of the reciprocity provisions in the banking sector as follows: requests for authorization by non-Community banks to be notified to the Commission by member states, but no automatic suspension; where equivalent treatment is not granted, the Commission may propose opening negotiations with the third country concerned; where national treatment does not give effective market access, the Commission may seek to limit or suspend new authorizations from the third country concerned in addition to opening negotiations.

Leon Brittan, Vice-President of the Commission responsible for Financial Services, said that: 'The proposed changes send a clear message to our trading partners. It will encourage banks from countries outside the Community to set up subsidiaries here. We welcome the establishment of their banks in the Community'.[57]

Undoubtedly, the concept of 'reciprocity' has been somewhat clarified by comparison with the original proposal, and the new clause in the revised draft directive states that there would be no automatic suspension of new authorizations from third-country banks by the Community. This modification, however, fails to respond to a number of concerns among the Community's trading partners.

First, the revised proposal requests third countries to grant the Community's credit institutions 'effective market access' and 'competitive opportunities comparable to those granted by the Community to non-EC banks ("equivalent treatment")', and makes clear that 'if the Commission find that a third country is not granting these opportunities to the Commission's credit institutions, it may propose to the Council to negotiate with the third country in question'. Second, the proposal requests third countries to grant the Community's institutions 'national treatment' and the same competitive opportunities as the third countries' own institutions, and provides that if the Community's institutions do not enjoy these opportunities, 'the Commission may limit or suspend new authorizations and acquisitions by a parent undertaking governed by the third country in question'.

There are several points of issue to be clarified. First, the definition of 'effective market access' is not clear. Second, while the Commission noted that the revised proposal 'makes clear that the "national treatment should really work in practice', it does not require third countries to provide 'national treatment' to the Community's institutions, but 'competitive opportunities comparable to those granted by the Community to non-EC institutions'.[58] In other words, the revised proposal still requests third countries to grant so-called 'mirror-image' reciprocity.

In addition, there is another very sensitive problem, that is the method by which the Community would judge the equivalence of access to markets: by the number of financial institutions investing in the other party's market, the gross business holdings or the net profit? Take as an example access to the Japanese financial market. The Commission and some member states still appear to be convinced that the Japanese financial market is very hard to penetrate, so foreign firms' share of total business in the market is very small and their profitability is low. While it is undeniable that their market share in Japan is small and their profitability low, it is hard to say whether their poor performance is due to Japan's heavily protected market.

Many barriers still remain in the Japanese market. In recent years, however, many administrative changes have been made to allow foreigners equal access to the market. Anthony Loehnis stresses that 'the bilateral talks between the United Kingdom and Japan held on financial matters in recent years have been very successful in terms of progress on access to Tokyo markets'.[59] Early in 1988, Ralph Ziegler, then First President of the Union Bank of Switzerland in Tokyo, also said that Japanese officials 'have achieved a lot in the last two to three years and have kept the spread of liberalization at the highest possible limit to be safe for Japan's financial system'.[60]

As a result foreign banks and securities houses are now finding the Japanese market much more open. According to Anthony Loehnis, among British financial institutions and their subsidiaries which have applied for securities licences in Japan, only two institutions have so far had their applications turned down. One of them failed owing to its own procedural mistake. He observes that one of the main reasons why the European share of the Japanese market is so small is that only very few European institutions had applied for Japanese licences.[61]

Other sectors into which the Commission is planning to introduce the reciprocity mechanism seem to have had similar problems to the banking sector. These sectors include other services such as transport; tele-communications; information services; investment; intellectual property rights; and government procurement sectors not covered by the GATT procurement code. Among them, to date, reciprocity provisions have been incorporated into the Directives or proposed Directives on Banking, Capital Movements and Public Procurement.

The Commission is examining the draft Investment Service Directive which may also make access to the integrated market conditional on reciprocity. In this connection, the Council Directive on Liberalization of Capital Movements stipulates that member states must endeavour to achieve the same degree of liberalization with non-member countries as has been attained within the Community. It indicates that this does not prejudice existing or subsequent provisions in related areas (right of establishment, financial services and admission of foreign securities to national capital markets), where the principle of reciprocity must be applied.[62]

In other service sectors too, the Commission makes it clear that it intends to eliminate the existing fragmentation of the Community markets, and emphasizes that whenever relevant Community rules do not exist, 'it will seek to arrange access for firms from non-member countries on the basis of the reciprocal opening up of the market in those countries'.[63] The Commission also says, on telecommunications for example, that 'it will propose that the reciprocal arrangements which have been and continue to be negotiated by the Member States should be analysed, and conclusions drawn for action at Community level'.[64]

Regarding government procurement, on 11 October 1988 the Commission issued two new directives on procedures for the award of public contracts – one covering water, energy and transport services, the other telecommunications.[65] These are not covered by the GATT code and are therefore excluded from existing directives constituting so-called 'excluded sectors'. The Commission indicates that for sectors covered by the GATT code, Community subsidiaries of non-member countries' firms will have the same access as Community firms, and suppliers not established in the Community will still be subject to the GATT code. But in the 'excluded sectors', the Commission states that it 'is prepared to negotiate with its partners access to the advantages of the internal market in order to ensure a balance of benefits'.[66]

The 'reciprocity' which the Community is planning to seek from third countries as a condition for access to the newly integrated market is still too vague. Since the proposed Second Banking Coordination Directive was sent to the Council, the Commission or Commission officials have suggested a number of possible criteria of reciprocity, including 'national treatment', 'competitive opportunities comparable to those granted by the Community to third country firms' (equivalent access or treatment) and 'an overall balance of concessions'. There have been, however, very few cases which referred to 'national treatment'. Kenzler, for example, said that 'the type of reciprocity requirement adopted by the Community would be close to "national treatment" for Community firms in third markets'.[67] Although the Commission noted in its revised proposal for a Second Banking Coordination Directive that 'the "national treatment" should really work in practice',[68] this does not, under the Commission's definition, mean that foreign firms would be given equality of competitive opportunity with domestic firms. That is, the Commission's definition is inconsistent with the principles of genuine national treatment and non-discrimination.

As far as the Community's statements or its officials' suggestions on this matter are concerned, the Community's reciprocity-based policy may be directed towards a narrow usage focusing on equivalent market treatment, in some cases even for a limited range of services and goods. Thus, it focuses judgment on a particular sectoral basis rather than recognizing an overall balance. It should, however, be understood that this is an issue of current negotiation in the Council of Ministers. Views within the Community are divided, and it is by no means clear at this stage what the outcome will be. The Community could adopt reciprocity mechanisms that were unilateral in nature and that could also be used as a means to make politically sure of arbitrary comparative advantage for the Community. Much depends on the outcome of the GATT round on services, but a narrow and defensive Community position would run a serious risk of retaliation from third countries, especially if it ignored GATT commitments.

6 Conclusion: The Tasks Ahead

On 19 October 1988, the Commission published an information memo entitled *Europe 1992: Europe World Partner*, which summarized the results of its internal discussions on the external dimension of the single market and explained the principles which would determine its external economic policy in the 1992 context as well as the approach it would adopt for implementing those principles. This document is the first fairly comprehensive explanation of the Community's external policy in the light of 1992. Its main points were reaffirmed by the European Council in Rhodes on 2-3 December 1988.

The Commission document stressed that 'the Community, whose role as the world's leading trading power is bound to become increasingly important once the single market is in place, will seek a greater liberalization of international trade,[1] and made it clear that 'the 1992 Europe will not be a fortress Europe but a partnership Europe'.[2] At the same time, 'the Community's aim is to strengthen the concept of mutual benefits and reciprocity'.[3]

Needless to say, the Commission indicated that its policy guidelines would be the two internationally accepted principles of trade policy contained both in the GATT and in OECD. The GATT, for example, envisages 'being desirous of contributing to . . . objectives by entering into reciprocal and mutually advantageous arrangements . . .'.[4] The GATT principle, however, implies global reciprocity, with the aim of maintaining an approximate balance of perceived advantages among trading partners operating under conditions of free competition.

An earlier version of the Community's position had been expressed by de Clercq, as the Community's chief delegate to the special session of the GATT contracting parties at Punta del Este in September 1986, at the launching of a new round of multilateral trade negotiations, the Uruguay round. He said:

One of the aims . . . is to ensure the mutual advantage of, and to bring increased benefits to, all participants. . . . The Community feels that many of the present

tensions affecting world trade find their origin in the fact that concessions negotiated between the various contracting parties have in reality not resulted in effective reciprocity. It is therefore essential that the Ministerial Declaration should
establish the objective of achieving a genuine balance in the benefits accruing to
the contracting parties from the GATT.[5]

The new issue which the Community put on the table was dubbed the
'balance of benefits' or 'Bob' clause. It was designed to correct the
enormous imbalances in global trade by denying the benefits of the new
round to nations which erected barriers to imports. From the outset, it was
known as the 'Japan clause', although it did not mention that country
specifically. During the Uruguay meeting, Japanese representatives fought
off the Community's move to have their trade policy obliquely attacked in
the final declaration and agenda. According to *The Times* of 24 September
1986, a Japanese minister actually used the term 'Japan-bashing' in front of
a large gathering of journalists, to describe the Com-munity's tactics. Eventually, the statement from Enrique Iglesias, chairman of the conference
(the Uruguay Foreign Minister), called on unnamed countries to tackle a
'growing disequilibrium' by changing their economic policies. He said: 'It
was common ground that growing disequilibrium in world trade constituted a serious problem and would need to be tackled by the countries concerned by various policy means including macroeconomic policies,
exchange rates, structural reforms and trade policies'.[6]

If the 'balance of benefits' means legal equivalence as regards
opportunities for market access and equal treatment within the market, it is
not incompatible with the principles of the GATT. This balance is exactly
what the Uruguay round is trying to achieve, by ensuring the opening of
the market and national treatment. The Community's concept, however, as
then explained by de Clercq, implied an equivalence of concrete economic
benefits or an equivalence of outcomes. At the same time, this seemed to
express the Community's fundamental attitude to the external dimension:
namely 'reciprocity' based on bilateral and sectoral balances of advantage
as outcomes, rather than an approximate balance of advantages in a
liberalization process.

The Community's arguments, therefore, gave the impression that it
regarded imports as a disadvantage and exports as an advantage. This, not
surprisingly, generated fears elsewhere that the Community's approach
was inconsistent not only with GATT principles, but with the basic
principles of a free market which rest on a free competition on a non-
discriminatory basis. In the GATT, it is important for contracting parties to
implement tariff reductions reciprocally and to maintain the equilibrium of
their burdens. However, if the Community attempted to make its trade
with a third country precisely balanced, for example balancing exports and
imports between them bilaterally, then it would be tending towards
'managed trade'. Precise balances of trade or of exports and imports are,
however, inconsistent with a process of free competition or liberalization.

Free competition under conditions of equal opportunities should over time produce the greater advantages – the basic principle of free trade. The Community appeared to be seeking not equality of opportunities, but equality of outcome.

The Community's tendency towards managed trade was evident in the invocation by some of its members of Article 35 of the GATT against Japan in the early 1980s. Article 35 provides for the non-application of the GATT between particular contracting parties, if either of them does not consent to its application to the other at the time of either becoming a contracting party. In 1955, when Japan became a GATT member, West European countries, including the United Kingdom, Belgium, the Netherlands and later France, invoked Article 35 in refusing to extend MFN treatment to Japan (see p. 14). At that time, West European countries harboured a strong fear of an aggressive Japanese export offensive and resented Japanese import restrictions. Early in the 1960s, these countries withdrew the application of Article 35 against Japan and replaced it by their own restrictions. Many of these restrictions still exist; at the end of 1988, there were 131 QRs in force, though the Commission notified Japan that the EC would soon lift 42 of them (see p. 67).

More than thirty years after the signing of the Treaty of Rome, and although the Treaty gives the Commission extensive competence on external trade matters, the Community still has no common trade strategy towards Japan. At trade talks between the two parties, Japan's negotiating partners have sometimes been governments and industries from EC member states, and not only the Commission. The remaining 131 QRs symbolize the results of the diffuse decision-making structure of the Community. Member states have retained considerable powers on trade matters, especially at the behest of those with protectionist tendencies. This ambiguous approach has been a long-established characteristic of the Community and has allowed strong protectionist elements to survive.

These protectionist elements and their discriminatory arrangements well predate the Treaty of Rome. They seem to derive, in part, from earlier relationships between member states and their overseas associates. Many of these agreements have been preserved and, in some cases, have been adopted by member states – for example, the preferential trading arrangements with the 66 African, Caribbean and Pacific (ACP) countries of the Lomé Convention and with EFTA. In its trade relations with the rest of the world, the EC has adopted discrimination as a norm, and against Japan in particular. David Henderson, chief economist at the OECD, has commented that 'one of the main constituent elements of a liberal trading system has thus been explicitly set aside'.[7]

These discriminatory tendencies are reflected in the current Community position which attaches much more importance to the advantages in the outcomes of trade than to the process of free competition or liberalization. To put it more bluntly, the Community has been tempted to seek bilateral reciprocity of trade outcome and to target those countries which have a bilateral surplus with it, as regards not only the general balance of trade but also the sectoral balances. This approach derives from French and Italian policy in particular; West Germany and the United Kingdom, by contrast, have generally supported the process of free competition. This discriminatory bias has become more and more conspicuous in the past few years, and is reflected in the concepts of 'balance of mutual benefits' and 'reciprocity'.

In July 1988, in a widely quoted speech, de Clercq stated: 'We see no reason why the benefits of our liberalization should be extended uni-laterally to third countries. We shall be ready and willing to negotiate reciprocal concessions with third countries, preferably in a multilateral context but also bilaterally. We want to open our benefits, but on the basis of a mutual balance of advantages in the spirit of the GATT'.[8]

This remark was taken at the time as an expression of the Community's fundamental position and seemed to confirm the evidence of existing EC trade practices.

There has been a strong sectoral theme to the push for a 'balance of mutual benefits' or 'reciprocity'. Many recent moves by the Community – for example, strengthening local content provisions, introducing new anti-dumping regulations or developing financial services (e.g. banking and investment services) – have called on third countries to demonstrate a 'balance of mutual benefits' or 'reciprocity' in individual product or service sectors, such as automobiles, electronics and other high technologies as well as financial services.

The Commission said in its information memo of October 1988 that 'the Community is not seeking sectoral reciprocity based on comparative trade levels'.[9] The directives proposed by the Commission on banking, invest-ment services and public procurement do, however, include reciprocity clauses. The reciprocity provisions of the Second Banking Coordination Directive, for example, even in their revised form of April 1989, stipulated that:

[Third countries grant] the Community's credit institutions market access and competitive opportunities comparable to those granted by the Community to non-EC banks . . .

The Community banks . . . enjoy national treatment and the same competitive opportunities as the third countries' own credit institutions and . . . the condition of effective market access has . . . been secured.[10]

The Community is tending towards a situation where economic and trade relations will no longer be determined by different countries' relative availability of labour, particular skills, technological sophistication or capital, or their ability to compete. Instead government intervention and the non-competitive attitude of Community firms will become decisive factors. Henderson points out that 'the Community has evinced a strong and continuing concern with sectoral and bilateral balances, particularly in its relation with Japan'.[11]

In the context of the 1992 programme, and given the poor competitiveness of some European industries, it is quite possible that the Community will strengthen its protectionist tendency. According to Henderson, the Community's trade policy, which has involved widespread recourse to protectionism and discrimination over the past two decades, 'is now more protectionist than it was fifteen to twenty years ago' and 'is not currently becoming less so'. He points out some 'obvious facts' as to why it would be unwise to expect the Community to change direction:

(1) the tendency to set aside liberal principles has become firmly entrenched;
(2) there is at present little visible evidence of a renaissance of free trade ideas in the Community; and
(3) all energies and attention are understandably directed towards the completion of the single market.[12]

This protectionist tendency is gaining ground throughout the Western world. Although United States officials frequently criticize the Community's attitude, its origin can be traced to the US in the mid-1970s. The world economy now urgently needs to resolve the dichotomy between the global system which it has so far been trying to sustain and regional approaches such as the Community's 1992 programme or the Free Trade Agreement between the United States and Canada. The concept of bilateral and sectoral 'balance of mutual benefits' or 'reciprocity' based on outcomes (so-called 'mirror-image' reciprocity) would hasten the regionalization of the world economy. The concept of 'reciprocity' based on an approximate balance of advantages within a pattern of free trade competition, by contrast, would serve to promote multilateralism and should not be passed over lightly. Gerard and Victoria Curzon have argued that the principle of reciprocity 'ensures that in any free trade, the "pain" of increased imports can be balanced, politically, with the prospective "pleasure" of increased exports, allowing some space for the government and civil service to represent the general interest somewhere in the midst of the fray'.[13]

It should, however, be pointed out that since early 1988, the general Community attitude towards third countries, and towards Japan in particular, has become unmistakably more constructive. As regards 'reciprocity', the Commission has sought to allay the fears of third countries, mainly the United States and Japan, that the concept would be used as an instrument of protectionism. It has thus significantly modified its position. In its statement setting out for the first time a comprehensive external policy strategy after 1992, the Commission stressed that the Community's concept of 'reciprocity' does not mean that all partners must make the same concessions.[14] In its amended proposal for a Second Banking Co-ordination Directive, it made clear that it was planning to inject more flexibility into the treatment of third country banks seeking the proposed Community-wide banking licence, by inserting a clause to the effect that the 'reciprocity' test will not be automatic.[15]

In April 1989, Martin Bangemann, Vice-President of the Commission, surprised the Community's automobile industry and member governments by proposing that the national quantitative restrictions on Japanese cars operated by five member states should be lifted in 1993, and that no Community-wide imports quota be introduced on them in their place.[16] West Germany, United Kingdom and the Netherlands all declared themselves in favour of Bangemann's proposal.[17] Dieter von Würzen, West German State Secretary for Economic Affairs, for example, stated that it was not practicable to adopt a Community-wide quota system for Japanese cars after 1992 and that such an arrangement would violate the GATT.[18]

Since then, France and Italy have separately abandoned their threats to block imports of Nissan cars assembled in the United Kingdom.[19] Moreover, in May 1989, the Commission adopted a proposal on overall Community strategy for the automobile industry, concluding that any attempt to dent the competitive challenge posed by Japanese-owned car plants in Europe by subjecting them to mandatory local content standards would violate international trade law.[20] The fundamental position of both Bangemann and Andriessen, who jointly drafted this proposal, is as follows:

(1) The Commission's position concerning investments from third countries should be to welcome them, whatever their origins.
(2) Within the limits of its powers, the Commission is bound to respect the OECD's guidelines on direct investments and it will abide by its commitments. In this regard, it has also to adhere strictly to Article 3 of the GATT which prescribes the principle of national treatment for imports. Should local content rules favour Community production over imported products, such rules would undoubtedly violate this GATT Article.[21]

It should be pointed out that the Commission showed for the first time a clear consensus in favour of extending the internal market approach of liberalization to the highly protected car industry.

In January 1989, the Confederation of German Industry (BDI) argued that 'the Community must exert constructive influence on the international trading system, especially under the GATT', and stressed that 'national import restrictions in the form of quotas, the tendency towards NTBs in the Community, and the introduction of "local content" regulations as already exist in some cases at national level would be just as fatal for the cohesion of the Community', and the extension of national restrictions to the entire Community 'would place European industry itself in fetters'.[22] These various moves indicate an important development of the Community's external strategy.

There remain, however, numerous hurdles, and it will not be easy to reverse the present trend towards protectionism and discrimination. In spite of its repeated definitions and redefinitions of 'reciprocity', the Commission has failed to calm third countries' fears that its proposals for the banking and the securities sectors may be designed to gain better than national treatment for the Community's firms in non-member countries and could result in discrimination against third countries' firms. Commenting on the amended proposal for a Second Banking Coordination Directive, for example, Sir Leon Brittan said that the EC would have to enter into negotiation with those partners which, while not actually discriminatory, were in practice less liberal than the EC.[23] Needless to say, this policy is inconsistent with the principles of national treatment.

According to *The Financial Times* of 3 May 1989, there is no sign that France, Italy or Spain are ready to dismantle their Japanese car import curbs unless they are promised EC restraints. Indeed, at one informal meeting of the Council of Ministers on 7 April 1989, French and Italian Industry Ministers 'defended the principle of reciprocity', and stressed that 'reciprocity will have to be demanded in Japan and Korea'.[24] The Commission itself does not rule out an 'additional limited interim period' beyond 1993, during which the Community would ask Japan to continue 'monitoring' its exports and to abide by a jointly agreed growth rate.[25]

Passive self-interest appears to have been the main reason why France and Italy abandoned their threats to restrict sales of Nissan cars made in the United Kingdom. The two governments found it difficult to impose special conditions, which turned out to be incompatible with Community rules, on the Nissan cars. Roger Fauroux, French Industry Minister, said: 'It is better to have Japanese cars than unemployed people'.[26] An Italian Foreign Trade Ministry official reiterated that Italy still considered the Nissan car made in the United Kingdom a Japanese, not a European car, because of 'the outstanding and unsettled issues of local content'.[27]

However, not only has the general stance of the Community begun to change, but, as already mentioned, there have also been signs of specific improvements in the past few years in relations between the Community and Japan. Whether calculated in dollars or in yen, the Community's exports to Japan have been steadily increasing, and growing faster than Community imports from Japan. The pace of Japanese direct involvement in the Community has been accelerating. There has been growing industrial collaboration between the Community and Japanese companies. This encouraging trend is due in part to the fact that Japan's economy has undergone a structural change from an export-oriented economy to one where economic growth is stimulated by internal demand. This structural change has encouraged West Europeans to take notice of the tremendous potential of the Japanese market and to make efforts to export to Japan.

Many economic frictions, however, still exist between the two parties. Both must try to make further efforts to accelerate the improvement in their relations and to fight protectionism in the world. It is imperative that the Community should not create any new barriers, and should reduce existing ones, vis-à-vis not only Japan but other third countries as well. It should do everything possible to make sure that the 1992 programme does not promote discriminatory or protectionist external policies towards third countries. Community firms have become more successful of late in gaining access to the Japanese market, but they need to make even more aggressive marketing and investment efforts.

As for Japan, its structure of trade and balance of payments have undergone a consistent and far-reaching change since the late 1960s (except during the two oil crises). There is now no truth in the claim that barriers against imports of manufacturers are lower in the United States and the Community than in Japan, if the following are taken into account: discriminatory import restrictions against Japan, VERs that the United States and some Community member states have formally or informally demanded from Japan and some developing countries, import restrictions under the MFA, etc.[28] Nevertheless, politicians, policy-makers and business circles, as well as the general public in the United States and the Community, still cling to the stereotyped image of a relatively closed Japanese market. No further evidence is needed than the US government's unilateral and high-handed decision in May 1989 to identify Japan as 'an unfair trading nation' under the Super 301 provisions of the 1988 Trade Act.

Japan, however, is not blameless. It seems to have little understanding of the fact that its economic activities, and its substantial trade surpluses in particular, have adverse effects not only on other countries, but also on the world economy as a whole. Japan has thereby jeopardized the free trade system, even though it has taken measures to correct the situation during the 1970s and 1980s.

The central problem concerns Japan's export-oriented economic and trade policies, implying the need for a more balanced integration of the Japanese economy with that of its main trading partners, including the Community. The most important medium and long-term task for Japan is to transform its export-oriented economic structure to one that is more balanced and gives greater emphasis to the social and economic infrastructure and to the people's standard of living. As a result of more than thirty years of rapid economic growth, a tremendous concentration of resources, both capital and human, has taken place in the productive sector. In April 1986, a report of the Maekawa Committee placed considerable emphasis on these points.[29]

As already stated, Japan's main trading partners, the United States and the Community in particular, have repeatedly asked it to make this structural adjustment. Moreover, elements within Japan's political circles welcome such foreign pressures on Japan, and the resulting liberalization of Japanese markets and economic restructuring. But there is a danger that Japan's main trading partners, the United States in particular, may use the situation to interfere in the internal affairs of a sovereign state. American pressure has aroused resentment among some Japanese who feel that the United States has been trying to influence their domestic institutions. The structural adjustment is a matter that the Japanese people and government must decide on, if they judge that their country's present export- oriented character is causing serious difficulties on the international scene.

But there is another problem. Japan's trading partners have complained that it has only been prepared to take economic and trade measures slowly, and only at some times and in some areas. Many foreign observers attribute this to a 'small country' or 'small power' mentality and regard it as an illustration of Japan's lack of the sense of international responsibility appropriate to a strong economic power. It can hardly be denied that since the Second World War, Japanese foreign policy has been markedly passive and reactive. The Japanese government has responded to foreign pressure by piecemeal individual measures. Its decision-making process is slow and based on consensus between all those involved in the negotiations. This makes an unfavourable impression on Japan's main trading partners who feel that the Japanese are at an advantage, taking more time to evaluate them and double-check their facts and figures.[30]

But the Japanese government has certainly made concessions to pressure from the United States. There are a lot of reasons why it has had to give in to US pressure in not only economic but also political, security and cultural relations. Japan both fears US retaliation against it and feels indebted to the United States for its security.

These concessions have only encouraged the United States to strengthen its pressure on Japan and tempted the Community to follow the Americans in restricting Japanese imports and pressing for changes in Japanese internal regulations and social customs.

Japan has to strive to maintain high economic growth at the same time as implementing further market liberalization measures resulting from structural economic reforms and continuing industrial and technological cooperation with third countries including the Community.

If the Community and Japan could work together for the stability of the free trade system, they would be on the way to solving their economic conflicts. They could also help the United States, which has moved further and further from liberal trade policies in the past two decades to set its economic house in order.

Notes

Chapter 1

1. The Commission of the European Communities sent the Council its White Paper *Completing the Internal Market* on 14 June 1985. The paper highlighted the Community's shortcomings and defects, and set out what needed to be done over the next seven years in order to create a single European market.
2. The Treaty of Rome was signed by France, West Germany, Italy, the Netherlands, Belgium and Luxembourg on 25 March 1957. It came into force on 1 January 1958.
3. I.e., with the Commission's White Paper *Completing the Internal Market*.
4. According to Franz H. J. J. Andriessen, Vice-President of the Commission, in a speech on 21 July 1989. The Commission has twice reduced the original 299 legislative initiatives: first to 286 (The Commission of the European Communities, *Third Report from the Commission to the Council and the European Parliament – On the Implementation of the Commission's White Paper on Completing the Internal Market*, Brussels, 21 March 1988), and then to 279 (Lord Francis A. Cockfield, the then Vice-President of the Commission Responsible for the Internal Market in a press conference on 9 November 1988).
5. 'It would be folly to try to fit them [the member states of the Community] into some sort of Identikit European personality'; 'My third guiding principle is the need for Community policies which encourage enterprises. If Europe is to flourish and create the jobs for the future, enterprise is the key'; 'The lesson of economic history in the 1970s and 1980s is that central planning and detailed control don't work'; 'Consider monetary matters. The key issue is not whether there should be a European central bank' (addressing the College of Europe on 20 September 1988); 'A Centralized European government would be a nightmare' (speech at a lunch given in her honour by the Luxembourg Prime Minister on 21 September 1988); 'I am never quite sure what it is, but if it means having a regulation on Community company law, something on worker participation, then I would oppose that particular thing' (press conference in Madrid on 23 September 1988).
6. Paolo Cecchini with Michel Catinat and Alexis Jacquemin, *The European Challenge 1992 – The Benefits of a Single Market* (Aldershot: Wildwood House, 1988). The so-called 'Cecchini report' provided the hard evidence that the failure to achieve a single market had been costing European industry dearly in

unnecessary costs and lost opportunities and that the completion of the internal market would regenerate European industry in both goods and services. The report foresees 'a major relaunch of the Community economy': a 4.5 per cent rise in the Community's GDP, a 6.1 per cent drop in consumer prices and an average improvement of member states' public finances of approximately 2.2 per cent of their respective GDPs.

7. Marie-Paule Donsimoni, Elisabeth Rocha and Stan Standaert wrote to *The Financial Times* of 12 April 1988 as follows: 'Studying the macroeconomic impact for the 12 EC countries, we find much smaller effects than those described in the Cecchini report. By 1995, we estimate that Community GDP will be boosted by 0.5 per cent (ECU 17.5 billion at 1987 prices) and employment will have risen by 300,000'.

8. Speech in London on 31 March 1989 (Commission typescript, p. 2).

9. On 1 January 1973, free trade agreements came into force between the Community and some EFTA member countries (Austria, Portugal, Switzerland and Sweden). Agreements with other EFTA members (Iceland, Norway and Finland) came into force later. These countries have not, however, participated in the Community's common policies.

10. The first joint meeting of ministers of all Community and EFTA member countries and representatives of the EC Commission, in Luxembourg on 13 April 1984, adopted a 'Declaration' to extend their cooperation by going beyond their free trade agreement with a view to creating a 'European Economic Space' (EES) covering the whole of the Community and the free trade zone.

11. Statement at the European Parliament, Strasbourg, 17 January 1989 (Commission typescript, p. 31).

12. Ibid., pp. 31, 32.

13. Helen Wallace and Wolfgang Wessels, *Towards a New Partnership: the EC and EFTA in the Wider Western Europe*, EFTA Occasional Paper No. 28, EFTA Economic Affairs Department, March 1989. It states : 'EFTA has had no real nuisance value for the EC, nor presented a need for the more sharply focused strategies that characterize the EC's links with the US and Japan' (p. 2).

14. On 4 August 1988, Peter McPherson, then US Deputy Secretary of the Treasury, said: 'the United States would find unacceptable measures that would discriminate against foreign companies already established' ('The European Community's internal market program: an American perspective', speech to the Institute for International Economics, Washington DC). According to *The Financial Times*, 26 October 1988, he also stated 'that resort to what he called "mirror-image" reciprocity would set the Community on a collision course with the United States'.

15. COM(87) 715 final. Proposal for a Second Council Directive on the Coordination of Laws, Regulations and Administrative Provisions Relating to the Taking-up and Pursuit of the Business of Credit Institutions and Amending Directive 77/780/EEC, OJ C84, 31 March 1988, the Commission; COM(89) 190 final. Amended Proposal for a Second Council Directive . . ., 29 May 1989, the Commission.

16. COM(88) 778-SYN 176. Proposal for a Council Directive on Investment Services in the Securities Field (OJ C43/7, 22 February 1989), submitted by the Commission to the Council, 3 January 1989.

17. COM(88) 729, submitted by the Commission to the Council, 21 December 1988.
18. COM(88) 823, submitted by the Commission to the Council, 22 December 1988.
19. The Commission, *Europe 1992: Europe World Partner*, Brussels, 19 October 1988, p. 2.
20. Declaration by the European Council, Rhodes, 2 December 1988.
21. *The Financial Times*, 8 April 1989.
22. Gardner Patterson, 'The European Community as a threat to the system', in William R. Cline (ed.), *Trade Policy in the 1980s* (Washington DC: Institute for International Economics, 1983), pp. 223, 234, 241.
23. For support of this view of mine, see Gerard and Victoria Curzon, 'Follies in European trade relations with Japan', in *The World Economy*, June 1987, p. 155.
24. Ministry of Foreign Affairs of Japan.
25. At the second round of informal consultations between the Community and Japan on residual QRs, Brussels, 17 March 1989 (press briefing by officials of the Japanese Ministry of Foreign Affairs in Brussels on 17 March 1989, and *International Herald Tribune*, 18 March 1989).
26. '1992: the impact on the outside world', speech by Willy de Clercq, then the Commissioner Responsible for External Affairs, in London on 12 July 1988 (Commission typescript, p. 5).
27. The Commission, *Europe 1992: Europe World Partner*, p. 3.
28. *The Financial Times*, 19 July 1988 and 5 October 1988.
29. Yutaka Kume, President of Nissan Motor, statement in Paris on 27 September ber 1988, quoted by *The Financial Times*, 28 September 1988.
30. *The Financial Times*, 28 September 1988.
31. The Commission, press release IP(89) 257, 18 April 1989.
32. On 22 June 1987 the Council adopted a Commission proposal for an amendment to the regulation of 23 July 1984 on production against dumped or subsidized imports from non-Community member states. The amended regulation enables an anti-dumping duty to be levied on products which would otherwise have been exempt because of having been assembled in the Community. The amended regulation lays down that the anti-dumping duty will be levied on products released into the Community market when assembly or production has been carried out by an enterprise which is related to or associated with any manufacturer whose exports of the same product are subject to a definitive anti-dumping duty; also when assembly or production was begun or substantially increased after the opening of anti-dumping proceedings; and when the value of parts or materials used in the assembly or production operation which originate in the country exporting the product subject to an anti-dumping duty exceed by at least 50 per cent the value of all other parts or materials used.
33. Declaration by the European Council in Rhodes, and The Commission, *Europe 1992: Europe World Partner*.
34. Andriessen, (as note 8), p. 3.
35. Declaration by the European Council in Rhodes.
36. Ibid.
37. The Commission, *Europe: 1992 . . .*
38. A White Paper delivered to the Commission by the Committee of Common

Market Automobile Constructors (Comité des constructeurs d'automobiles du Marché Commun, CCMC), and the liaison Committee of the EC Motor Vehicle Manufacturing Industry (CLCA), two main Community car lobby groups, (*The Financial Times*, 2 March 1988).

39. The Commission, *A Competitive Assessment of the European Automotive Industry in View of 1992*, Brussels, 14 October 1988.
40. Jacques Calvet, chairman of Peugeot, 20 February 1989, quoted in *The Times*, 21 February 1989.
41. Ministry of Finance of Japan.
42. Speech in Kanazawa on 27 October 1987, quoted by *Japan Times*, 28 October 1987.
43. Statement in Osaka on 5 April 1988, quoted by *Japan Times*, 8 April 1988.
44. On 31 May 1989, the Commission decided to propose that national restrictions – both QRs and VERs – used by France, Italy, Spain, Portugal and the United Kingdom to protect their car producers against Japanese competition should be eliminated by 1992, and that during a second phase starting in 1993 and for a clearly set and limited period, Japan would continue to monitor the growth of its exports at Community level (*Europe*, 16/17 May 1989; *The Financial Times*, 1 June 1989).

Chapter 2

1. Albrecht Rothacher, *Economic Diplomacy between the European Community and Japan 1959–1981* (Aldershot: Gower, 1983), p. 327.
2. *Japan and America Today* (Stanford: Stanford University Press, 1953), pp. 66–7.
3. James E. Meade, *Japan and the General Agreement on Tariffs and Trade*, The Joseph Fisher Lecture in Commerce (Adelaide: University of Adelaide, 1956), p.11.
4. *The Economist*, special supplement, 1 and 8 September 1962.
5. *Nippon Times*, 30 May and 16 June 1956.
6. The OECD Council unanimously voted to invite Japan to join on 26 July 1963, and the Japanese Diet ratified the membership on 9 April 1964.
7. Average annual growth ratios (1960–72): Japan – 10.3; France – 5.7; Italy – 5.0; West Germany 4.6; UK – 2.7, Netherlands – 5.1 (GATT, *International Trade 1976/77*, p. 75).
8. *Bulletin of the European Communities*, December 1969, p. 17.
9. Ibid., p. 4.
10. IMF, *Direction of Trade Statistics Yearbook, 1958–62, 1962–6, 1968–72*, Washington DC.
11. Ibid.
12. The Commission of the European Communities, Note B10 (70)78, aux bureaux nationaux, Brussels, 25 September 1970.
13. Article 113, paragraph 3, The Treaty of Rome.
14. Council decision No. 69/494 (OJ L326, 16 December 1969).
15. The Commission, *Sixth General Report on the Activities of the Communities 1972* (Brussels: 1973), sec. 472.
16. Council Regulations No. 288/82, 5 February 1982 (OJ L35, 9 February 1982). The Council adopted the regulation establishing the 'new common imports system' applicable to all third countries with the exception of state trading

countries. One of its principal elements was the new version of the rules authorizing certain member states to maintain (in principle until the end of 1984) some national measures, mainly with regard to Japan (automatic licences, import declaration formalities, national surveillance over imports of specified products, etc.).

17. IMF, *Direction of Trade Statistics Yearbook, 1968–72 and 1970–76.*
18. Campbell Adamson, then Director General of the CBI, in a speech in Nottingham on 14 October 1971 (*The Times*, 15 October 1971).
19. Meeting with the Commission of the Community, Brussels, 25 October 1971, and with UNICE and the CBI, Brussels, 26 October 1971.
20. Brussels, 26 October 1971.
21. Press conference, 26 October 1971 (*The Guardian*, 27 October 1971).
22. Announcement by the Electronic Machinery Industry Association of Japan, 5 June 1972.
23. *The Times*, 20 September 1972, reported: 'The Japanese electronics industry is to apply price controls to exports of black-and-white television sets and tape recorders from mid-October, the Electronic Machinery Industry Association said today [19 September 1972]. West Germany would be excluded as it had raised an objection to the inauguration of a cartel to control imports of Japanese products . . . The Japanese industry has already applied such a cartel from August to the three Benelux countries under the guidance of the Ministry of International Trade and Industry [of Japan].'
24. Brian Hindley, 'Voluntary export restraints and the GATT's main escape clause', *The World Economy*, November 1980, p. 313.
25. For example, at preparatory meetings for the official negotiations on a common trade agreement (Tokyo, February 1970) or at high-level consultations (Brussels, June 1973) between the Japanese government and the Commission.
26. *The Times*, 14 July 1972.
27. A letter from the West German Economics Ministry to the High Cartel Authority in West Berlin, 17 August 1972.
28. 16 October 1972.
29. OJ C111, 21 December 1972: 'Recently and with increasing frequency the Japanese industries have been preparing measures, either independently or with their European counterparts, to limit the imports of Japanese products into the Community or control them in other ways regarding quantities, price, quality, etc.

   'The Commission deemed it necessary to draw the attention of those concerned to the fact that under Article 85, paragraph 1 of the EEC Treaty any inter-company agreements, any agreements between company groups and any concerted practices apt to have ill effects on inter-Member State trade and aimed at or resulting in hampering, hindering or distorting fair competition within the Common Market are incompatible with the Market and prohibited. The fact that some or all of the companies involved have their headquarters outside the Community does nothing to change application of this provision insofar as the effects of agreements, decisions or concerted practices infringe on the Common Market territory.

   'The Commission has recommended those concerned to notify it, as laid down by the provisions and rules for competition in the EEC Treaty, of such agreements, decisions and practices so as to determine whether they can be deemed compatible with the rules. At the same time, the Commission will closely follow developments in the sectors concerned and will propose as required appropriate trade policy measures to clear up problems arising.'

30. *The Financial Times* 15 November 1973.

31. France and the Benelux countries told Jean-François Deniau, then the head of a Commission delegation in charge of negotiations with Japan that they would prefer not to have a common Community agreement with Japan at all than have to renounce their individual safeguard clauses (*Le Monde*, 21 February 1970).

32. *The Financial Times*, 8 February 1974.

33. Speech at the Harvard Club in Tokyo on 9 February 1978.

34. Tokyo, 24 February 1978 (*International Herald Tribune*, 25/6 February 1978).

35. *New York Times*, 24 January 1970.

36. Speech by Deniau at the Foreign Correspondents Club, Tokyo, quoted by *New York Times*, 17 February 1970.

37. *The Times*, 18 July 1970.

38. *The Financial Times*, 9 July 1971.

39. *International Herald Tribune*, 9 July 1971.

40. For example, François-Xavier Ortoli, then President of the Commission, proposed a common trade agreement with a safeguard clause at the talks in Tokyo with Yasuhiro Nakasone, then Japanese Minister of International Trade and Industry (*Japan Times*, 19 February 1974).

41. Talks between Nakasone and Ortoli (ibid.).

42. IMF, *Direction of Trade Statistics Yearbook, 1964–68, 1968–72*.

43. This agreement, concluded by Japan and the Community in Tokyo on 12 May 1976, became effective on 1 April 1977.

44. The Japanese government, on 26 November 1976, gave the Commission its reply to the Community's demand that it rectify the huge trade surplus in their bilateral trade.

45. The Commission, *Japan: Consultations in Train and Envisaged – Working Paper of the DGI – On the Agenda for 509th Meeting of the Commission on 21.3.1979, Item 11*, dated 19 March 1979.

46. Working report, International Finance Bureau, Japanese Ministry of Finance, circulating May 1977 (*The Financial Times*, 22 June 1977).

47. The Commission, *Japan: Consultations in Train and Envisaged*.

48. *The Financial Times*, 29 January 1981; *International Herald Tribune*, 12 June 1981.

49. Report to the European Parliament's External Trade Committee, 22 September 1980.

50. Press conference in Paris on 10 October 1980 (*The Financial Times*, 11 October 1980).

51. Radio interview, Paris, 3 February 1981 (*The Financial Times*, 4 February 1981).

52. *Japan Times*, 1 February 1981.

53. Associated Press, 4 February 1981.

54. *Bulletin of the European Communities*, 5, 1981, sec. 134–138.

55. West German Motor Industry Federation, July 1980.

56. Otto Graf Lambsdorff said on 10 June 1981 that an 'understanding' had been reached with Japanese government and car industry officials for Japan to limit car exports to West Germany in 1981 to no more than 10 per cent above the 1980 level (*The Financial Times*, 11 June 1981).

57. Japan agreed to cut its 1981 car shipments to Belgium and Luxembourg by 7 per cent from the 1980 level and to hold exports to the Netherlands to the 1980 level (*International Herald Tribune*, 12 June 1981; *Japan Times*, 16 June 1981).
58. OJ L54, 28 February 1981.
59. Commission study on the structures situation and the outlook for the Japanese machine tool industry (*Europe*, 4 April 1981).
60. Ibid.
61. Commission study on the structures situation and the outlook for the Japanese colour television sector (*Europe*, 2 April 1981).
62. *Sunday Times*, 13 April 1980.
63. *The Financial Times*, 10 April 1980.
64. *The Financial Times*, 8 April 1980.
65. *Journal Officiel de la République française*, 22 October 1982.
66. *The Financial Times*, 19 November 1982.
67. *The Financial Times*, 3 November and 22 December 1982.
68. *International Herald Tribune*, 5 November 1982; *The Financial Times*, 5 December 1982.
69. Interview, *Les Echos*, 29 November 1982.
70. *International Herald Tribune*, 5 November 1982.
71. *The Financial Times*, 8 November 1982.
72. *The Financial Times*, 14 February 1983.
73. *The Financial Times*, 15 February 1983.
74. The Commission, *Analysis of the Relations between the Community and Japan*, 15 October 1985. There are differences between Community and Japanese statistics.
75. Dentsu Japan Marketing Advertising, *Case Studies on Successful Penetration of the Japanese Market by Foreign Products*, Tokyo, Fall-Winter, 1982.
76. The Commission, *Analysis*.
77. Commission-document in which the Community formally put a request that proceedings against Japan should be opened under Article 23 of the GATT, *Europe*, 9 April 1982.
78. The Commission, *Analysis*.
79. Endymion Wilkinson, *Japan versus Europe – A History of Misunderstanding* (Harmondsworth: Penguin Books, 1983), p. 71.
80. 'Japan – economic power and partner for the Common Market', *Bulletin of the European Communities*, December 1969, pp. 17–20.
81. *Bulletin of the European Communities*, December 1969, pp. 244–65.
82. Masamichi Hanabusa, *Trade Problems between Japan and Western Europe* (Westmead: Saxon House, 1979), p. 6.
83. The Commission, *Japan: Consultations in Train and Envisaged*.
84. *Europe*, 8 and 9 April 1982.
85. *The Financial Times*, 13 April 1983.
86. The Commission, *EC-Japan Relations: Arguments and Counter-arguments*, Brussels, April 1982, p. 5.
87. The Commission, *Analysis*, p. 19.
88. OECD, *Japan – Economic Surveys*, 1988, p. 78.
89. Gary R. Saxonhouse, 'Japan's intractable trade surpluses in a new era', *The World Economy*, September 1986, p. 246.
90. *The Financial Times*, (leading article), 30 March 1979.

91. US Trade Representative (USTR), 1982, pp. 58–9, quoted by Bela Balassa and Marcus Noland, *Japan in the World Economy* (Washington DC: Institute for International Economics, 1988), p. 57.
92. European Parliament, *On Trade Relations between the EEC and Japan*, 3 June 1981.
93. Jean-Pierre Lehmann, 'Agenda for action in issues in Euro-Japanese relations', *The World Economy*, September 1986, p. 261.
94. Gerard and Victoria Curzon, 'Follies in European trade relations with Japan', *The World Economy*, June 1987, p. 166.
95. The Commission, *Analysis*, p. 16.
96. Ibid., p. 17.
97. Ibid.
98. Saxonhouse, 'Japan's intractable trade surpluses', p. 241.
99. Gary R. Saxonhouse, 'The micro- and macro-economics of foreign sales to Japan' in William R. Cline (ed.), *Trade Policy in the 1980s* (Washington DC: Institute for International Economics, 1983).
100. The Commission, *Analysis*.
101. *Asahi Shimbun*, 30 June and 7 July 1985. In the United States there were a few reports on this matter. For example, the *International Herald Tribune* reported on 29 July 1985 that 'Secretary of State George Shultz has joined academics and economists in calling on Japan to change policies that favour savings over investment'.
102. OECD, *Japan Economic Surveys*, 1985, pp. 45, 46.
103. *The Economist*, 15 February 1986.
104. Saxonhouse, 'Japan's intractable trade surpluses', p. 253.

Chapter 3

1. Gerard and Victoria Curzon, 'Follies in European trade relations with Japan', *The World Economy*, June 1987, p. 155.
2. Endymion Wilkinson, *Japan versus Europe: A History of Misunderstanding* (Harmondsworth: Penguin Books, 1983), p. 82.
3. R. Baloon, 'A European views the Japanese', in *The Wheel Extended*, special supplement, No. 2, 1978, pp. 1–5.
4. Alexander Cairncross and others, *Economic Policy for the European Community* (London: Macmillan, 1974), p. 2.
5. Walter Hallstein, *Europe in the Making* (London: G. Allen & Unwin, 1972), p. 19.
6. Frans A. M. Alting von Geusau, *Beyond the European Community* (Leyden: A. W. Sijthoff, 1969), p. 21.
7. Marshall Darrow Shulman, *Beyond the Cold War* (New Haven: Yale University Press, 1966), p. 3.
8. Resolution adopted by the Ministers of Foreign Affairs of the member states of the European Community for Steel and Coal (ECSC) at a meeting at Messina on 1 and 2 June 1955.
9. Hallstein, *Europe*, pp. 18, 19.
10. *Rapport des chefs de délégation aux ministres des affaires étrangères*, Brussels, 21 April 1956.

11. Albrecht Rothacher, *Economic Dipolmacy between the European Community and Japan 1959–1981* (Aldershot: Gower, 1983), pp. 117, 118.
12. Hallstein, *Europe*, pp. 253, 254.
13. Ibid., p. 254.
14. G. C. Allen, *A Short Economic History of Modern Japan* (London: Macmillan, 1981), p.163.
15. Wilkinson, *Japan versus Europe*, p. 166.
16. GATT, *International Trade, 1972, 1974, 1976/77*.
17. Wilkinson, *Japan versus Europe*, p. 68; OECD, *Main Economic Indicators, Historical Statistics, 1955–1971* (OECD Statistical Office, 1973).
18. Statement by French delegate to the GATT, 1975, in GATT Doc. L1164, p. 25.
19. Wilkinson, *Japan versus Europe*, p. 178.
20. 'Japan – economic power and partner for the Common Market', *Bulletin of the European Communities*, December 1969, pp. 17–20.
21. Jean-Piere Lehmann, 'Agenda for action on issues of Euro-Japanese relations', *The World Economy*, September 1986, p. 263.
22. *The Competitiveness of the Community Industry*, Document of the Commission Services, 1982, pp. 7–13, 37–9.
23. Ibid., p. 11.
24. The Commission Document III/387/82, 5 March 1982, p. 12.
25. *The Competitiveness of the Community Industry*, p. 8.
26. Ibid., pp. 24, 25.
27. Ibid., p. 9.
28. Silvio Leonardi summed up the situation as follows: 'Unlike Japan, the EEC as a whole has been unable over the past decade sufficiently to increase its trade in manufactured products to offset the higher costs of raw materials, particularly oil. Nor has it adopted the measures needed to achieve a balance in respect of services and transfers – unlike the USA which, moreover, has energetically pursued the goal of "active adjustment" and influenced the development of other countries by transferring part of its industrial capacity abroad'. 'The competitiveness of the Community industry', in Giovanni Leodari and Antonio Mosconi (eds), *Strategies and Policies of the European Economic Community to Improve the Competitiveness of European Industry* (Milan: St B, 1984), pp. 23, 24.
29. *The Financial Times*, 7 December 1981.
30. See Leonardi, 'The competitiveness of the Community industry', p. 23.
31. Hans J. Dörsch and Henri Legros, *Les Faits et les Décisions de la C. E. E. 1958–64* (Brussels: Presses universitaires de Bruxelles, 1969), p. 434.
32. *The Financial Times*, 1 May 1963; *Le Monde*, 15 May 1963.
33. Tokusaburo Kosaka (then Director-General of the Japanese Economic Planning Agency) in an interview with *Newsweek*, 16 April 1979.
34. 'Community trade policy towards Japan', *Bulletin of the European Communities*, 7/8, 1980, pp. 11–13.
35. *Japan Times*, 29 December 1956.
36. *Le Monde*, 19 and 20 June 1960.
37. *Le Monde*, 24 and 25 December 1961.
38. Duhamel (at that time Director-Général of the Centre national du commerce extérieur), *Le Monde*, 27 April 1962.
39. *Neue Züricher Zeitung*, 5 July 1961.

40. *ANSA*, 10 October 1980; *Guardian*, 11 October 1980; *The Financial Times*, 24 September 1986; etc.
41. *Sunday Telegraph*, 13 April 1980; *The Financial Times*, 18 May 1983; etc.
42. *International Herald Tribune*, 19 April 1972.
43. *Der Spiegel*, 14 August 1972.
44. *The Financial Times*, 1 October 1977.
45. *The Financial Times*, 10 April 1980.
46. *The Financial Times*, 18 May 1983.
47. *The Economist*, 9 June 1973.
48. Gardner Patterson, 'The European Community as a threat to the system', in William R. Cline (ed.), *Trade Policy in the 1980s* (Washington DC: Institute for International Economics, 1983), p. 226.
49. *Case 6/64 Costa v. ENEL (1964) E.C.R. 1141*, 15 July 1964.
50. *Case 22/70 (AETR) Commission v. Council (1971) E.C.R. 263*, 31 March 1971.
51. Anthony Parry and James Dinnage, *Parry and Hardy – EEC Law*, (London: Sweet & Maxwell, 1981), 2nd edn, p. 421.
52. Maurice Flory, 'Commercial policy and development policy' in The Commission, *European Perspective – The Thirty Years of Community Law*, Brussels, 1983, p. 378.
53. Parry and Dinnage, *Parry and Hardy*, p. 425.
54. Ralf Dahrendorf, 'Possibilities and limits of a European Community foreign policy', in Steven J. Warnecke (ed.), *The European Community in the 1970s* (New York: Praeger Publishers, 1972), p. 118.
55. *Case 1/75 (1975) E.C.R. 1353*, 11 November 1975.
56. *Case 1/78 (1978) E.C.R. 2151*, 14 November 1978.

Chapter 4

1. *On the Move* (Japanese government official bulletin), October 1988, pp. 1, 2; Ryutaro Komiya and Motoshige Itoh, 'Japan's international trade and trade policy', in Takeshi Inoguchi and Daniel I. Okimoto (eds), *The Political Economy of Japan* (Stanford: Stanford University Press, 1988), pp. 206, 216; and Bela Balassa and Marcus Noland, *Japan in the World Economy* (Washington DC: Institute for International Economics, 1988), pp. 49, 50.
2. Gary R. Saxonhouse and Robert M. Stern, 'An analytical survey of formal and informal barriers to international trade and investment in the United States, Canada and Japan', in *Proceedings of a Conference on the United States, Canada and Japan: Trade and Investment Nexus* (Chicago: University of Chicago Press, 1988), quoted by Mordechai E. Kreinin, 'How closed is Japan's market? Additional evidence', *The World Economy*, December 1988, p. 529.
3. Bela Balassa and Marcus Noland write that: 'On the whole, tariff rates on non-agricultural products in Japan approximate those of the European Community and the United States. Before the latest reductions, Japanese tariffs averaged 0.5 per cent on raw materials, 4.6 per cent on semi-manufactures, and 6.0 per cent on finished manufactures, compared with 0.2, 3.0 and 5.7 per cent, respectively, in the United States, and 0.2, 4.2, and 6.9 per cent in the European Community. . . . These data are unweighted averages. The overall weighted tariff average is now lower in Japan than in the United States and

the European Community, but Japan's average is considerably biased downwards because of the large imports of duty-free raw materials', (*Japan in the World Economy*, pp, 49, 50).

4. *On the Move*, October 1988, pp. 1, 2.
5. Ibid., p. 3.
6. Ibid., pp. 5, 6.
7. Ibid., pp. 6, 7.
8. Ibid, p. 11.
9. Ibid.
10. 'Japan's place in a unified Europe: the Japanese view', speech in Glasgow on 17 March 1989 (official typescript, p. 4).
11. See pp. 96–108.
12. Brussels, 17 March 1987.
13. Luxembourg, 25 April 1988.
14. Press conference by Genscher when President of the Council, 25 April 1988, quoted by *Europe*, 27 April 1988.
15. The Commission of the European Communities, *Analysis of the Relations between the Community and Japan*, Brussels, 15 October 1985, p. 4.
16. Council Regulations (EEC) No. 288/82 on Common Rules for Imports, 5 February 1982 (OJ L35, 9 February 1982). Title 1, General principles, Article 1: '1. This regulation shall apply to imports of products covered by the Treaty orginating from third countries, except for: textile products subject to specific common import rules; products originating in State-trading countries; products originating in the People's Republic of China; products originating in Cuba. 2. Importation into the Community of products referred to in paragraph 1 shall be free, and therefore not subject to any quantitative restrictions, without prejudice to . . . quantitative restrictions for the products listed in Annexe 1. . . .'
17. Article 1, paragraphs 1 and 2.
18. Council Decision 69/494, OJ L326, 1969.
19. Article 11, paragraph 2 (c).
20. Article 12.
21. Article 20.
22. Article 21.
23. Statement by Michihiko Kunihiro, Japanese Deputy Minister for Foreign Affairs, at the CBI-Chatham House conference, London, 11 October 1988. The text was printed in *The World Today* (Royal Institute of International Affairs, London), February 1989, pp. 29–31.
24. The Commission, *EC-Japan Relations, Arguments and Counter-arguments*, April 1982.
25. The Commission, *The Trade Policy of the Community and Japan: A Re-examination*, Brussels, 15 July 1980, p. 5.
26. 'Community trade policy towards Japan', *Bulletin of the European Communities*, July/August 1980, p. 12.
27. The second round of informal consultation between the Community and Japan on residual QRs, Brussels, 17 March 1989. Press briefing, officials of Japanese Ministry of Foreign Affairs, Brussels, 17 March 1989. On the same day, the Commission announced that 'the Community offered abolition of around 68 of the 156 QRs maintained by member states (press release IP(89)

174). But these figures include the 25 QRs which Portugal abolished on 12 April 1988.

28. Press briefing by officials of the Japanese Ministry of Foreign Affairs, Brussels, 17 March 1989; and press briefing by a Commission spokesman, 17 March 1989; *International Herald Tribune*, 18 March 1989.

29. The Commission, *Europe 1992: Europe World Partner*, Brussels, 19 October 1988, p. 3.

30. Peter McPherson in a speech to the Institute for International Economics, Washington DC, 4 August 1988.

31. United States Government Interagency Task Force on the EC Internal Market, *An Initial Assessment of Certain Economic Policy Issues Raised by Aspects of the EC Program – Public Discussion Document*, December 1988, p. 11.

32. Ibid., p. 12.

33. Ibid.

34. Early in January 1989, the Commission fixed at 14,000 passenger cars (including station wagons and racing cars) the number originating in Japan that Italy will have to allow in during 1989 by 'Community free circulation' through other member states. Beyond that figure Italy will be able to apply the safeguard clause of Article 115 of the Treaty and refuse further imports. It should be noted that at the beginning of 1989 the Italian authorities received requests for the indirect import via other member states of 108,298 units. Italy is thus entitled to refuse most of them. The safeguard measure does not apply to off-road vehicles. This quota of 14,000 units is apparently additional to the quota directly opened by Italy to Japan (*Europe*, 12 January 1989). In 1988, Italy had a quota of 10,500 units for indirect imports.

35. *The Financial Times*, 29 September 1988.

36. *The Financial Times*, 13 October 1988.

37. *The Financial Times*, 26 September 1988.

38. Giorgio Rampa, President of the CLCA and of the Italian Association of Motor Vehicle Manufacturers (ANFIA), *Europe*, 9 December 1988.

39. Ibid.

40. On 9 November 1988 (*The Financial Times*, 10 November 1988).

41. *The Financial Times*, 19 November 1988.

42. Michihiko Kunihiro, Statement.

43. *The Financial Times*, 19 May and 1 June 1989; *Europe*, 16/17 May and 1 June 1989.

44. The Commission, *A Competitive Assessment of the European Automotive Industry in View of 1992*, Brussels, 14 October 1988, p. 28.

45. Ibid., p. 22.

46. The Commission, *The European Automobile Industry*, Brussels, 16 June 1981.

47. *The Independent* and *The Times*, 27 January 1989.

48. *The Financial Times*, 8 November 1988.

49. *The Financial Times*, 25 January 1989.

50. DRI, *DRI World Automotive Forecast Report*, London, November 1988.

51. Rampa, op. cit. (no. 213).

52. 'Bill Hayden, Combative manufacturing director, Ford of Europe', *The Financial Times*, 25 January 1989.

53. A White Paper, CCMC and CLCA, quoted by *The Financial Times*, 2 March 1987.

54. *The Financial Times*, 14 October 1986.
55. *The Daily Telegraph*, 30 September 1988.
56. *The Financial Times*, 30 September 1988; *Europe*, October 1988.
57. *The Financial Times*, 1 October 1988.
58. *The Financial Times*, 18 October 1988; *Europe*, 19 October 1988.
59. *Europe*, 19 October 1988.
60. *The Financial Times*, 9 March 1989.
61. *Europe* and *The Financial Times*, 4 November 1988.
62. *The Times*, 5 December 1988.
63. The Commission, press release IP(89), 257, 18 April 1989.
64. *The Financial Times*, 2 May 1989.
65. *The Financial Times*, 3 May 1989.
66. 31 May 1989 (*Europe*, 16/17 May and 1 June 1989; *The Financial Times*, 19 May and 1 June 1989.
67. *Japan Times* and *The Financial Times*, 27 January 1989; and *Japan Times* and *The Financial Times*, 14 July 1989.
68. At the Paris motor show, 27 September 1988 (*The Financial Times*, 28 September 1988).
69. Ibid.
70. *The Financial Times*, 31 October 1988.
71. *The Financial Times*, 5 October 1988.
72. *The Financial Times*, 5 October 1988.
73. *The Financial Times*, 1 October 1988.
74. *The Financial Times*, 29 September 1988.
75. An interview, quoted by *The Financial Times*, 13 October 1988.
76. No. 1761/87, 22 June 1987.
77. *Daily Telegraph*, 27 January 1989.
78. Kyoto, 13 March 1973, effective from 25 September 1974.
79. OJ L100, 1975, p. 2.
80. Council Regulation No. 802/68, 27 June 1968, OJ L148/1, 28 June 1968.
81. Commission Regulation No. 2632/70, 23 December 1970, OJ L279:35, 1970; Commission Regulation No. 861/71, 27 April 1971, OJ L95/11, 1971.
82. Council Regulation No. 1761/87. 22 June 1987.
83. US Government Task Force, *An Initial Assessment*.
84. Michihiko Kunihiro, Statement.
85. Council Regulation No. 1761/87, 22 June 1987, OJ L167, 26 June 1987.
86. Council Regulation No. 2176/84. 22 July 1984, OJ L201, 30 July 1984.
87. 'Tai-o toshi masatsu' (Strains caused by Japan's increased investments in the Community), *Nippon Zaigai Kigyou Kyoukai*, April 1988, p. 117; *The Financial Times*, 4 February 1988.
88. Council Regulation No. 2423/88, 11 July 1988, OJ L209, 2 August 1988.
89. *The Financial Times*, 4 February 1987.
90. Council Regulation No. 1788/77, OJ L196, 3 August 1977.
91. OJ C146, 12 June 1979, and OJ C207, 17 August 1979.
92. Otto Grolig and Peter Bogaert (attorneys in the Brussels Office of Baker and McKenzie), 'The Newly-amended EEC anti-dumping regulation: black holes in the Common Market?', *Journal of World Trade Law*, Geneva, December 1987, p. 85.
93. *EC-Japan Relations* (Commission Communication to the Council), 6 March

1986, p. 11.
94. 'Fortress Europe is a myth', *The Financial Times* 19 January 1989.
95. 'Dumping and the Far East trade of the European Community', *World Economy*, Trade Policy Research Centre, London, December 1988, p. 446.
96. OJ L176, 6 July 1985.
97. *The Financial Times*, 10 May 1988.
98. *The Financial Times*, 22 September 1988.
99. *The Financial Times*, 20 December 1988.
100. *The Financial Times*, 20 December 1988.
101. Statement by CJPrint, *The EC Commission's Anti-dumping Proceeding Concerning Imports of SIDM Printers originating in Japan*, released a few days before the Commission's announcement of a provisional anti-dumping duty on Japanese printers (26 May 1988), CJPrint typescript, pp. 1, 2. According to *The Financial Times* of 29 June 1988, CJPrint sent a note to the Commission citing several examples, including that of the Honeywell model L32CQ1, which was priced at DM 2,492, being compared with Brother M1509, the Epson FX1000, and the Oki ML193, all of which were priced under DM 2,000. It says, however, that the Honeywell products are rated as heavy duty machines, lasting 7,000 to 9,000 hours and with a head life of 500 million characters, but the Japanese products are in general intended for personal computers, with a life of 5,000 to 6,000 hours and a head life of 100 million characters. It concludes that it is like comparing a Rolls Royce with a Fiat Uno.
102. OJ L130, 26 May 1988.
103. Council Regulation No. 2423/88, Article 2 (9) and (10).
104. Christopher Norall, 'New trends in anti-dumping practice in Brussels', *World Economy*, March 1986, pp. 101, 102.
105. Clifford Chance, *EEC Dumping Law – An Introductory Guide* (London, 1987), p. 9.
106. Council Regulation No. 2423/88, Article 2, H. 'Dumping Margin' (b).
107. Chance, *EEC Dumping Law*, pp. 9, 10.
108. *The Financial Times*, 12 February 1987.
109. OJ L239, 26 August 1986.
110. *The Financial Times*, 27 May 1988.
111. Al Springsteel (Analyst, Dataquest), *The Financial Times*, 27 May 1988.
112. *Summary of Arguments of the Preliminary Submission on the Issue of Injury Delivered to the EC Commission on September 30, 1987, on behalf of the CJPrint and Relevant Trade Organizations*, CJPrint telex, 27 May 1988. It states: 'their [Japanese and EC manufacturers] different strategies have been reflected in their development of technology and markets. Japanese manufacturers have been responsible for the many significant developments in SIDM printer technology since the early 1980s, most particularly in terms of developing a 24-pin SIDM printer head for improved printing quality, establishing home-computer and IBM-PC compatibility, and improving the cost-effectiveness of production methods. . . . Meanwhile, most EC producers continued to restrict their SIDM printer business to developing SIDM printer technology and markets for niche computers primarily in the high-end segment . . .'.
113. 5 March 1989 (Keidanren typescript).
114. *The Financial Times*, 10 May and 25 October 1988.
115. 'Fair practice, not protectionism', *The Financial Times*, 21 November 1988.
116. 'Fortress Europe is a myth'.

117. Brian Hindley, 'The design of fortress Europe', *The Financial Times*, 6 January 1979.
118. Brian Hindley, 'Correcting the defects of EC dumping regulations', *The Financial Times*, 24 January 1989.
119. OJ L33, 4 February 1989.
120. 10 February 1989.
121. OJ L148, 28 June 1968.
122. *Europe*, 11 February 1989.
123. OJ C194, 2 August 1985. Initiation of proceedings concerning imports of photocopiers originating from Japan.
124. OJ L239, 26 August 1986. Provisional anti-dumping duties.
125. *Europe*, 6/7 February 1989.
126. *The Financial Times*, 10 February 1989.
127. *The Financial Times*, 10 February 1989.
128. 'Japan's place in a unified Europe: the Japanese view', speech in Glasgow on 17 March 1989.
129. OJ L240, 31 August 1988.
130. Council Regulation No. 3017/79.

Chapter 5

1. Statement, 23 June 1987, *Europe*, 26 June 1987.
2. Letter to the heads of state and top officials of all member states and the President of the Commission, 5 March 1987 (Keidanren typescript).
3. United States Government, *Completion of the European Community Internal Markets*, December 1988, p. 13.
4. *The Financial Times*, 4 and 12 February 1987, 5 March 1987.
5. *The Financial Times*, 4 February 1987.
6. *Nihon Keizai Shimbun*, 11 October 1988.
7. *The Financial Times*, 9 March 1988.
8. Willy de Clercq, 'Fair practice, not protectionism', *The Financial Times*, 21 November 1988.
9. 'Tai-o toshi masatsu' ('Strains caused by Japan's increased investment in the Community'), *Nippon Zaigai Kigyou Kyoukai*, April 1988, p. 58.
10. *The Financial Times*, 18 November 1988.
11. 'Tai-o toshi masatsu', p. 63.
12. Although 1987 investment statistics have already been announced (see Table 30), detailed figures as shown in Tables 28 and 29 are not yet available for 1987. Consequently this chapter uses figures up to March 1987, the end of FY 1986.
13. Japanese Ministry of Finance; see Table 26.
14. *The Financial Times*, 1 February 1989.
15. Muneoki Date, 'Japan's place in a unified Europe: The Japanese view', speech in Glasgow, 17 March 1989, p. 8.
16. *The Independent*, 19 April 1989.
17. JETRO, *Japanese Enterprises in Europe – A Survey Report on Management*, Tokyo, 1984. This report was the first comprehensive survey of Japanese manufacturing companies and joint ventures in Western Europe conducted by JETRO

about profitability, labour relations, management techniques and relations with local business partners.

18. The Commission of the European Communities, *EC-Japan Relations*, Commission communication to the Council, Brussels, 6 March 1986, p. 10.
19. *The Financial Times*, 11 September 1986.
20. The Commission, *EC-Japan Relations*, p. 10.
21. *The Financial Times*, 21 April 1982, 24 November 1982.
22. de Clercq, 'Fair practice'.
23. Don Pinchbeck, 'Japanese investment in the UK', speech in Glasgow on 17 March 1989.
24. Pinchbeck, 'Japanese investment', pp. 6, 7 (Epson typescript).
25. Ibid.
26. Date, 'Japan's place', p. 7.
27. French Electronics Industries Association, *Annual Report*, November 1988; *The Financial Times*, 18 November 1988.
28. *The Financial Times*, 27 February 1989.
29. *The Times*, 21 February 1987.
30. Cores Europe, *European Community 1992* (London, 1988).
31. Willy de Clercq, '1992: the impact on the outside world' speech in London on 12 July 1988 (Commission typescript, pp. 2, 3).
32. The Commission, *Europe 1992: Europe World Partner*, Brussels, October 1988, p. 2.
33. Anthony Parry and James Dinnage, *Parry and Hardy – EEC Law* (London: Sweet & Maxwell, 1981), 2nd edn, p. 263.
34. Ibid., p. 276.
35. William R. Cline, ' "Reciprocity": a new approach to world trade policy?', in William R. Cline (ed.), *Trade Policy in the 1980s* (Washington DC: Institute for International Economics, 1983), p. 121.
36. Business Roundtable, 'The statement of the Business Roundtable task force on international trade and investment on reciprocity in trade', New York, 19 March 1982.
37. Brian Hindley and Eri Nicolaides, *Taking the New Protectionism Seriously* (London: Trade Policy Research Centre, 1983), p. 63.
38. *Washington Post*, 7 May 1982.
39. Cline, 'Reciprocity', p. 131.
40. The Commission, *Europe 1992: Europe World Partner*, p. 2.
41. de Clercq, '1992: the impact', pp. 6, 7.
42. Peter McPherson, speech at the Institute for International Economics, Washington DC, on 4 August 1988.
43. United States Government, *Completion of the European Community Internal Market*, p. 2.
44. 'The external implications of the single European market: a view from Japan', Statement to the CBI-Chatham House conference, London, 11 October 1988 (typescript, p. 7).
45. At the CBI-Chatham House conference, London, 11 October 1988. See *The Financial Times*, 12 October 1988.
46. COM(87) 715 final. Proposal for Second Council Directive on the Coordination . . . of Credit Institutions and Amending . . ., and COM(89) 190 final. Amended Proposal for a Second Council Directive.

47. COM(88) 778-SYN 176. Proposal for a Council Directive on Investment Services in the Securities Field.
48. OJ C26/01, Proposal for a Council Directive for the implementation of Article 67 of the Treaty – Liberalization of Capital Movements, and OJ C26/02, Proposal for a Council Directive 72/156/EEC on Regulating International Capital Flows and Neutralizing their Undesirable Effects on Domestic Liquidity.
49. Statement to the United Kingdom House of Lords Select Committee on the European Communities, 7 February 1989.
50. *The Financial Times*, 8 November 1988.
51. Press briefing in London on 12 July 1988; *The Financial Times*, 13 July 1988.
52. *Euromoney*, December 1988, p. 47.
53. COM(87) 717 final. Comments on Articles, (e) Third country institutions, Article 7, pp. 7, 8.
54. London, 9 September 1988; *The Financial Times*, 10 September 1988.
55. The Commission, *Europe 1992: Europe World Partner*, p. 4.
56. Statement, ref. P/89/15, Commission, 13 April 1989.
57. Ibid.
58. Ibid.
59. Statement to the United Kingdom House of Lords Select Committee on the European Communities, 7 February 1989.
60. *Euromoney*, February 1988, p. 34.
61. Statement to the United Kingdom House of Lords Select Committee on the European Communities, 7 February 1989.
62. OJ C26/02, Article 1, paragraph 1.
63. The Commission, *Europe 1992: Europe World Partner*, p. 4.
64. Ibid.
65. COM(88) 377 (Water, energy and transport service) and COM(88) 378 (Telecommunications).
66. The Commission, *Europe 1992: Europe World Partner*, p. 3.
67. The CBI-Chatham House conference.
68. Ref. P/89/15/.

Chapter 6

1. Commission typescript, p. 2.
2. Ibid., p. 1.
3. Ibid., p. 2.
4. Preface.
5. *Bulletin of the European Communities*, September 1986, p. 15.
6. Statement by the chairman of the ministerial meeting, 20 September 1986. (*Basic Instruments and Selected Documents, 1985–86*, The contracting parties to the GATT, June 1987, p. 29).
7. Group of Thirty, *1992: The External Dimension* (London, 1989), p. 15.
8. *External aspect of . . .*, Commission typescript, p. 3.
9. The Commission of the European Communities, *Europe 1992: Europe World Partner*, 19 October 1988, p. 2.
10. COM(89) 190 final. Amended Proposal for a Second Council Directive on the Coordination of Laws, Regulations and Administrative Provisions Relating to

the Taking-up and Pursuit of the Business of Credit Institutions and Amending Directive 77/780/EEC, the Commission, 29 May 1989. Title 2A Reciprocity, Article 7.

11. Group of Thirty, *1992: The External Dimension*, p. 15.
12. Group of Thirty, *1992: The External Dimension*, p. 14.
13. Gerard and Victoria Curzon, 'Follies in European trade relations with Japan', *The World Economy*, June 1987, p. 174.
14. The Commission, *Europe 1992: Europe World Partner*, p. 2.
15. COM(89) 190 final. Amended Proposal.
16. Informal Council of Industry Ministers, San Sebastian (Spain), 7 April 1989, quoted by Reuters, 7 April 1989, and *Europe*, 10/11 and 12 April 1989.
17. Informal Council, *Europe*, 10/11 April 1989.
18. Informal Council, Reuters, 7 April 1989.
19. The Commission, Press release IP(89) 257, 18 April 1989;*The Financial Times*, 2 May 1989.
20. 31 May 1989, *Europe* and *The Financial Times*, 1 June 1989.
21. *Europe*, 16/17 May 1989.
22. Bundesverband der Deutschen Industrie (BDI), *Completion of the Single European Market – Consequences for the European Community's External Economic Relations*, January 1989, pp. 1, 10, 11.
23. Statement, ref P/89/15.
24. *Europe*, 12 April 1989.
25. *Europe*, 16/17 May 1989; *The Financial Times*, 19 May and 1 June 1989.
26. *The Financial Times*, 3 May 1989.
27. *The Financial Times*, 2 May 1989.
28. Ryutaro Komiya, and Motoshige Itoh, 'Japan's international trade and trade policy' in Takeshi Inoguchi and Daniel I. Okimoto (eds), *The Political Economy of Japan* (Stanford: Stanford University Press, 1988), p. 216.
29. The Maekawa Committee was commissioned in October 1985 by Nakasone, then Japanese Prime Minister, to make recommendations on the structural adjustment of Japan's economy. On 7 April 1986, it released its findings, the 'Maekawa Report'.
30. *On the Trade Relations between the EEC and Japan*, European Parliament working document No. 1-240/81, 3 June 1981, p. 19.

Index

Act
  Foreign Investment Review 81
  Omnibus Trade 6
  Single European 2
  Trade 111
Action Program 55, 58–9
Adamson, Campbell 131
administrative guidance 35–6
AEG-Telefunken 28
aero industry 41, 60
Aerospatiale 60
African, Caribbean and Pacific (ACP)
  countries 120
agreements
  bilateral 65
  common trade 131
  Free Trade 122, 128
  industry-to-industry 70
  'self-limitation' 20, 21, 49, 69, 133
  see also arrangements
Agt. Andrew van 11
Air Liquide 32
Andriessen, Frans H.J.J. 2–3, 123, 127
anti-dumping rule 82–4 *passim*, 95, 96,
  103, 104, 129, 140
Arrangements
  Long Term (LTA) 20
  Multi-Fibre (MFA) 20, 48, 125
  Short-Term 20
assembly plants, 'screwdriver' 8,
  82–94, 95, 104, 108
Austin Rover 75
Australia 13, 23
Austria 23, 69, 103
automobile manufacture
  criteria for 'local content' 8–9
  exports to Japan 22–3
  industry, wages in 44

large-scale production of 41–2
Nissan case 76–81
protectionist policy 49, 51, 68–71
quotas 138
restrictions on 49, 58, 123
tax on 60
understanding between Japan and
United Kingdom 48

balance
  of benefits 61, 119
  of mutual benefits 121–2
  of payments 15, 23, 66
ball bearings, 21, 83
Bangemann, Martin 78, 123
Bank of England 113
Bank of Switzerland, Union 115
barriers
  fiscal 2
  non-tariff (NTBs) xii, 10, 22, 32–3,
  36–7, 55, 123
  tariff xii, 110, 16, 53, 55–8, 69, 119,
  136
  technical 2
  trade 6, 65, 136
Barron, Derek 76
Beecham company 32
Benelux countries 15, 16, 19, 20, 26,
  49, 50, 51, 65, 70, 131
Bentsen, Lloyd (US Senator) 6
Bluebird cars 76, 78–9
BMW company 70
Bogaert, Peter 83
Bretton Woods 12
Brittan, Leon 114, 124
Brussels 17, 24
butter production 80

Cable and Wireless 60
Calvet, Jacques 108
Canada 24, 81
Cecchini, Paolo 2, 127–8
CCMC 71
Chance, Clifford 137
China 13, 137
CJPrint (Committee of Japanese
   Printers) 86
Cline, William R. 110
Cockfield, Lord Francis A. 127
commercial policy 53–4, 64
competitiveness (in trade) 40–8, 49
computer printers, serial impact dot
   matrix (SIDM) 83, 85, 86, 88–9,
   140–1
Confederation of British Industry
   (CBI) 17, 131
consumer
   demand 37
   interests of 94
   needs 35
convention on the simplification and
   harmonization of Custom Procedures 80
cotton 20
Council
   of Europe 10, 11
   of Ministers 113, 117, 124
   for Mutual Economic Assistance
   (CMEA) 3
currency
   single European 2
   ECU 3, 5, 92, 96, 97, 128
   yen 96, 106
Curzon, Gerald and Victoria 122, 129
customs 54

Dassault-Breguet 60
Data Resources International (DRI) 74,
   76
Date, Muneoki 85, 92, 99, 108
de Clerq, Willy 84, 103, 106, 109, 111,
   112, 113, 118, 119, 121, 129
Delors, Jacques 3, 78
Deniau, Jean-François 132
Denmark 30, 64, 69
Directive(s)
   on Coordination of Laws, Regulations etc. 128, 144
   on Investment Services 6
   on Liberalization of Capital Movements 112, 116, 143
   on Life Assurance 6

   on procedures for award of public
   contracts 6, 116
   on Second Banking Coordination 6,
   11, 112–17 *passim*, 121, 123, 124
distribution system 34–5
Doko, Toshio 22
Dole, Robert US Senator 110
DRI *see* Data Resources International
'dumping' of manufactures 8, *see also*
   anti-dumping rule

Economist, The 14–15
economy
   Japanese 15
   of United Kingdom 15
   of Western Europe 7
   world 24, 43
electrical household appliances 67
electronic industry
   in European Community 27–9, 51,
   85, 108
   in Japan 36
   restrictions on 20
Electronic Machinery Industry Association 131
Epson UK 106
Europe 1992: Europe World Partner 118
European
   competitiveness, declining 40–8, 49
   Court of Justice 29, 52, 53
   dilemmas 40–54
   Free Trade Association (EFTA) 3, 5,
   120, 128
   influence 40
   Machine Tool Confederation
   (CECIMO) 27
   Parliament 3, 53, 108, 132
   responses, defensive 48–54
European Community
   Council of 10, 11, 49, 82, 114, 118,
   130–1
   declaration by xi
   Directorate General for Competition
   18
   Directorate General for External
   Affairs 18
   Economic and Financial Affairs Division 114
   law 64–5
   Japanese investment in 75, 95–108
   policy 50, 51–2
   recession in 24
   rules 78
   for Steel and Coal (ECSC) 134

see also Treaty of Rome
EUROPRINT (Committee of European printer manufacturers) 86
export restraints, voluntary (VERs) 7, 10, 17–18, 28, 51, 68, 125
exports
  of automobiles 22–3, 104
  changes in 47
  Community 16, 30, 45, 61
  dependence on 55
  Japanese 10, 16–17, 20–2, 24–32, 43, 66, 67, 71, 120
  of manufactured products 45
  price 90

Fauroux, Roger 79, 124
Fiat 69, 74, 76, 77, 79
Financial Times, The 28–9, 30, 51, 90, 92, 103, 124, 128
Finland 69
Fitchew, Geoffrey 114
Ford Motor Company 25, 75, 76
foreign
  exchange reserves, Japanese 13, 14, 15
  exchange shortage 42
  investment in Europe 75, 81, 95–108
  securities companies 60
  trade policy 40
Free Trade Agreement 122, 128
France
  attitude to Japan 13, 15, 50–1, 97
  automobile industry 25–6, 74, 108
  and the Japanese market 112
  and the Nissan case 76–9, 99
  ownership of television sets 28
  protectionist policy of 21, 69, 108
  quantitive restrictions 64, 69
  restricted imports 16, 20, 28–9, 49, 71, 99
  trade negotiations 19, 65
  VTR anti-dumping regulations 28–9, 49
Fujitsu 86

GATT *see* General Agreement on Tariffs and Trade
General Agreement on Tariffs and Trade (GATT)
  agricultural measures 58
  anti-dumping committee 82, 84–7, 90
  European Community and 33

extension of measures 63, 109, 116–17
  and the Foreign Investment Review Act 81
  government procurement code 36
  integrated markets 5
  Japan's accession to 7, 13–14
  local content requirements 80
  protectionist measures 16, 19, 120
  and QRs 65
  reciprocal agreements 118–19
  restrictionist measures 20
  rules 68, 110
  spirit of 26, 121
US leadership of 6
  violation of 78, 123
General Motors 74
Generalized System of Preferences (GSP) 56
Geneva 33
Genscher, Hans-Dietrich 63
German Industry, Confederation of (RDI) 123
Ghidella, Vittorio 69, 79
Giraud, André 25–6
Greece 69
Grolig, Otto 83
gross domestic product (GDP) 2, 15, 39, 128
gross national product (GNP) 10, 15, 32, 41, 43–4
Grundig company 28, 30, 51

Haferkamp, Wilhelm 24
Hallstein, Walter 40–1, 42–3
Hanon, Bernard 25
Henderson, David 120, 122
high technology products 45, 47
Hindley, Brian 84, 88, 90–1
Hitachi company 51, 96
Hoechst company 32
Honda Motor 51, 69, 75, 76, 97, 104
housing 38–9

Iglesias, Enrique 119
Imperial Chemical Industries (ICI) 32
import(s)
  comparison of 24
  Community 15–16, 66, 71, 109
  Japanese 11, 30–2, 55, 59–60, 62, 71
  liberalization 57–8
  quotas 8, 9, 74
  of raw materials 60–1
  restrictions on 7, 21, 28, 48

rules 7, 11, 137
  of vehicles into Japan 72–3
Independent, The 99
India 43
industries
  automobile 8, 9, 22–3, 24–6, 41, 44,
    48, 49, 51, 58–9, 60, 67, 68–76, 81,
    123, 138
  Community 48
  European 14, 41
  Japanese 8, 9, 14, 15, 22
InfoMarkt 86
integrated circuits (ICs) 36, 91
International Herald Tribune 30, 132
investment in manufacturing 48,
  95–108 *passim*
Ireland 64, 69, 96, 103
Italy
  automobiles 68–9, 77, 97
  criteria for local content 76, 78, 104
  French imports to 51
  granting of MFN status to Japan 13
  nationalism 99
  negotiations with Japan 19
  and the Nissan case 78
  production losses 74
  and reciprocity 113
  restricted imports 16, 29, 64, 71
  right of derogation 50

Japan
  'bashing' 119
  car import curbs 124
  Committee of Japanese Printers
    (CJPrint) 86
  Federation of Economic Organiza-
    tions (Keidanren) 17–18, 22, 89, 95
  financial market 115
  foreign policy 126
  law 22
  low import propensity 32–9
  Ministry of: Construction 39;
    Finance 23–97; Foreign Affairs 26,
    129; International Trade and Indus-
    try (MITI) 35–6, 131, 132
  negotiator 52
  occupation by United States 42
  sales offensive 22
  structural reforms in 55–64
  structure of trade 125
  survey of manufacturing companies
    142

JETRO 99, 104–5, 106–8, 142
Jobert, Michel 29

Kawana, Yutaka 79
Keidanren *see* Japan, Federation of
  Economic Organizations
Korea 124
Krenzler, Horst G. 84, 90, 91, 112, 116
Kume, Yutaka 79
Kunihiro, Michihiko 71, 81, 112
Kyoto confectioner 18

Lambsdorff, Count Otto 29, 132–3
Land Rover Santana 75
Le Havre 28
Le Monde 51
Lehmann, Jean-Pierre 44
Leonardi, Silvia 135
Levy, Raymond 69, 79
Libya 16
Loehnis, Anthony 113, 115
Lomé Convention 50, 120
Luxembourg Declaration (1984) 3

McPherson, Peter 68, 128
McRae, Norman 14–15
machine tools 27
Maekawa Committee 125, 144
management, worker participation in 2
market
  closed 32, 55
  consumer 22, 30
  development 42
  disruption 16
  foreign 9
  integration, consequences of 4,
    108–9
  internal 78, 127
  Japanese domestic 10, 13, 32–3,
    35–6, 70, 125
    penetration 26
    share of 27, 48, 88
    single European 1–12, 61, 67–8, 71,
      118
  'marketing, orderly' 17, 19
Mazda cars 69
Meade, James 14
Mercedes-Benz 70
Messina 41
MFA *see* arrangements multi-fibre
MFN *see* nation, most-favoured

'mirror-image' 5, 9, 111–13, 122, 128
Mitsubishi company 69
Miyazawa, Kiichi 18
Moto Guzzi 51
motor cycles 51, 67
MTN *see* trade negotiations, multi-lateral
Mullard company 51

Nakasone, Yasuhiro 38–9, 132
nation, most-favoured (MFN) 7, 13–14, 15, 16, 65, 110, 120
Netherlands, the 13, 19, 103
Nippon Telegraph and Telephone Corporation (NTT) 112
Nissan Motor 8, 25–6, 69, 70, 74–5, 76–81, 97, 99, 104, 108, 123, 124
Nixon, Richard US President 17, 22
non-tariff barriers (NTBs) xii, 10, 22, 32–3, 36–7, 55, 123
Norway 69
NTB *see* non-tariff barriers
nuclear weapons 40

oil
    crisis 11, 12, 15, 22, 44, 135
    price increases 24
Olivetti company 32, 108
Organization of Economic Coopera-tion and Development (OECD)
    chief economist of 120
    Council 130
    electronics industry in 36
    exports of member countries 45, 47
    guidelines 123
    imports of member countries 24
    Japanese membership of 15
    membership of 35
    savings in 38
    trade policy of 109, 118
Ortoli, François-Xavier 132

Paris 28, 29
Parliament, European 3, 53, 108, 132
Patterson, Gardner 52
payments, balance of 15, 23, 66
Peugeot-Citroen 51, 76, 79
Pinchbeck, Don 106
Philips company 28, 30, 51, 108
photocopiers 91, 92
Poitiers incident 28, 29, 30, 99, 103
Portugal 69, 96

protectionism 5, 6, 24, 25, 29, 51, 69, 82
productivity 45, 46
Punta del Este Declaration 65, 118

QRs *see* restrictions, quantitive
quasi-NTBs 32, 33
quota system 28, 43, 69, 71, 78
radios 66, 80
Rampa, Giorgio 70–1
Reagan, Ronald US President 111
reciprocity 6, 8, 9, 108–17 *passim* 121, 122–3, 124
Renault cars 25, 51, 69, 75, 79, 108
restrictions, quantitive (QRs)
    administration of 54
    Community policy on 50, 120, 130
    discrimination 64–8
    effects on Japanese exports 16
    on Japanese exports 20–1, 55
    on Japanese imports 32, 56–8, 59
    maintenance of 63
    promise to lift 7–9, 130
    residual 58, 60
Rhodes, European Council meeting xi, 11, 118
Ricoh Electronics Inc (REI) 92, 94
Right of Establishment 110
Rover company 75, 104
Ruggiero, Renato 97
rules of origin 91–4

sales 45, 77, 87
Samsung 96
San Francisco 13
savings, household 37–9, 134
Saxonhouse, Gary R. 37
Scotch whisky 60
'screwdriver' assembly plants 8, 82–94 *passim*, 95, 96, 104, 108
services trade 9
Shell Oil Company 32
Shulman, Marshall Darrow 41
Shultz, George 134
Sicily 41
Siemens company 32
Silver Seiko 96
South Africa 13
South Korea 48, 96
Soviet Union
    attitude to European Community 3
    expansionism of 40–1

Spaak, Paul-Henri 41
Spain 16, 64, 69, 71, 74, 78
steel 17, 20, 23–4, 48, 106
Suntory company 99
Suzuki company 75
Sweden 16
Switzerland 16, 69

Tamura, Hajime 95
Tanaka, Kakuei 20
tariff(s)
   average 55
   barriers xii, 53
   high 10, 69
   increase in 16
   Japanese reduction in 55–8
   rates 136
   reductions 119
   US 137
tax
   income 38
   internal 60, 85
   trade 65
   value added (VAT) 2
   see also tariff(s)
telecommunications 60, 112, 116
television sets 27–8, 51, 80, 96
textiles 20, 42, 43, 48, 51, 67
Thatcher, Mrs Margaret MP 2
Thomson-Brandt company 28, 51
Tietmayer, Hans 113
Times, The 119, 131
Tokyo 14, 18, 24, 52, 55, 60, 115, 131
Tokyo Electric 86
Toyota Motor 69, 70, 75, 97, 99
trade
   agreements 16, 17, 49
   attitude to Japanese 14
   balance of 47
   between Japan and the Community 62
   conflict 42
   deficit 22
   development of 30–2
   figures 30
   free 9, 120
   gap 18, 23
   Investment Measures (Trims) 81
   law 123
   negotiations 9, 18–19
   negotiations, multilateral (MTN) 33
   policy 10, 51–2, 80

practices 9
preferences 120
regulation of 54
relations, post-war 12–39
restraints 26
surplus 23, 44, 55, 61, 63
US Omnibus Act 6
with EFTA, US and Japan 5
Treaty
   of Commerce, Establishment and Navigation 14
   of Rome: Articles of 53–4, 65, 66, 113, 138; authority of Commission 52; authors of 2; entry into force 6, 68; free-trading rules of 29; provisions of 21; Right of Establishment 110; signing of xi, 64, 120, 127; single European market 1; violation of 78
San Francisco Peace 13
Triumph Acclaim 76, 104

Union of Industries of the European Communities (UNICE) 17
United Kingdom
   reciprocity policy 110
   relations with EC members 5, 68
   Senate 6
   tariffs 55, 137
   Trade Act 111
   trade with Japan 17, 20, 22, 33, 38, 42–3, 60, 63
   trilateral relationship with Europe and Japan 12
Uruguay 9, 63, 81, 118, 119
Ushiba, Nobuhiko 18

VERs see export restraints, voluntary
video cassette recorders (VCRs) 92, 99, 103
   video tape recorders (VTRs) 28, 30, 49, 51, 80
Volkswagen 70, 75
von Würzen, Dieter 123

wages 44, 46
Wallace, Helen 5
War
   cold 40
   Korean 14
   Second World 1, 6–7, 12, 13, 15, 22, 36, 97, 126

Wessels, Wolfgang 5
West Germany
  automobile industry 69, 70
  durability test on automobiles 58
  granting of MFN status to Japan
    13–14
  cotton industry 43
  French accusations against 29
  import policy 21
  and Japan 14, 20, 50, 51, 64, 65, 71,
    96–7, 99, 115
  market share 74
  motor industry 48, 69, 76–81
  Nissan motor plant 25–6, 76–81, 124
  opposition to Japan joining GATT
    13
  photocopier proposals 92
  row with France 76–81 *passim*

United States
  active adjustment 135
  attitude to the Community 3, 95,
    111–12, 122, 128
  automobile industry of 58
  Congress 33, 110
  exports 61
  imports 125

Japanese investment in 74, 104
and Japanese trade policy 10, 13,
  125–6
labour force 41
market 22
Omnibus Trade Act 6
ownership of television sets 28
productivity 45
and protectionism 81
quota system 28
recession in 24
incentives 103
and Japanese market 97, 112
Japanese opinion of 18
Japanese pressure on 28
market 21
market share 74
and reciprocity 113
removal of restrictions on Japanese
  imports 15
restricted imports 16, 21, 64
and VTR restrictions 30

Yugoslavia 23

Ziegler, Ralph 115